The Miraculous Life of
St. Bernadette Soubirous
and the Message of Hope of
Our Lady of Lourdes

Includes the most striking miracles of St. Bernadette.

ANNA GARAVITT

I dedicate this book to each of my readers. I pray for you every day.

MESSAGE TO THE READER

Dear reader, first of all I would like to thank you for buying my book. I would like to begin by telling you more about myself and my literary inspirations. My name is Anna Garavit, I was born in Portugal, in a very Catholic family, I attended a private Catholic school and my education included religious instruction. I am a nun in a convent in Lisbon, I have had the opportunity to make several pilgrimages to the holy places where the Virgin Mary has appeared and I have personally experienced several incredible events in these places. For these reasons, I have taken on the task of writing in the best possible way about the events in which our Heavenly Mother has appeared on earth.

I have written several essays, analyses and texts in which I have summarized the most important information of the various apparitions, all because I have become a very devout woman since I had the experience of discovering the love of God and the Virgin Mary.

For many years I kept all my writings in storage and they were just gathering dust, but I decided to share them with the world because there is no reason or sense to keep them archived. There is a lot of information that is unknown to many authors, but when you read so much, you realize that there are different truths and they all complement each other.

I hope that my publication can fill you with peace, love of God, fascination and desire to learn more about this subject, as it did me more than ten years ago.

I would also like to humbly ask you to support me by giving me a comment or review of this publication, this is the best thanks I could receive.

I hope we can meet again in one of my other publications.

Sincerely,

Sister Anna Garavitt

INDEX

INTRODUCTION

The life of Saint Bernadette is the story of a poor and simple girl. She was fourteen years old and looked twelve. She was not physically developed. She had asthma. She could not read, write or speak French. She spoke only the local language, patois. She barely knew the Our Father, the Hail Mary, and the Creed; she did not know the catechism and had not yet made her First Communion. Nevertheless, God chose her to be Mary's messenger and to tell the world that she was the Immaculate, as the Pope had solemnly proclaimed four years earlier.

The Virgin Mary appeared to him 18 times from February 11 to July 16, 1858. Since the apparitions, her life has changed considerably. First, because many people wanted to see her and talk to her. Second, because she wanted to become a religious. She was admitted to the hospice of Lourdes as a student and then, in 1866, she finally entered as a religious of the sisters who ran the hospice: the Sisters of Charity and Christian Instruction of Nevers.

As a nun, she sanctified herself by the daily fulfillment of her religious duties and by accepting her sufferings for the conversion of sinners. As a child she suffered from asthma and later from a cancerous tumor in her knee. Never complaining, she fulfilled her mission in the silence and solitude of her bed in the infirmary, where she spent much of her short life.

Her life, obscure and hidden at first glance, was before God that of a giant of holiness. Therefore, after her death, God glorified her and made her body appear incorruptible.

May her life inspire us on the path of holiness and may we offer our sufferings for the salvation of the world. And may our love for Mary lead us to love Jesus, present in the Eucharist, more and more each day.

LOURDES

It was a small town with a population of 4,510 according to the 1861 census. There was a police station, an imperial procurator and a justice of the peace. In the famous castle of Lourdes, which overlooked the town, there was a military detachment and an ammunition depot. On the slopes of the nearby mountains, there were marble and slate quarries where many workers worked. Others were engaged in farming and raising animals such as sheep, rams and goats, as there was good pasture.

At the time of the apparitions, Emperor Napoleon III reigned in France and Pius IX was Pope of the Catholic Church. After the apparitions, a beautiful basilica of three churches was built, and today Lourdes is a city known throughout the world. It welcomes millions of pilgrims every year and is a beacon of faith, light, love and peace for all.

THE SOUBIROUS FAMILY

It all started with a tragedy. On June 1, 1841, Justin Castérot, the owner of the Boly mill, died at the age of 41. His wife, Clara Labit, was left a widow with four daughters and a son, and he had no work to support them. He thought that the eldest, Bernarda, 18 years old, could marry a miller to take over the work of the mill. Among the many suitors, only one was a miller, Francis Soubirous. He was 34 years old, but he preferred the second daughter, Louise, 17 years old, of medium height, blond and blue-eyed. The mother accepted and they were married on January 9, 1843. Neither signed the marriage certificate, a sign that they did not know how to write. They had nine children, five of whom died in infancy. The last one did not survive his birth, but only a few minutes, and therefore was not registered in any registry. Therefore, some authors speak of only eight children.

Both husbands took over the mill and paid rent to the widow Castérot, who continued to live in the mill house with her other children. Mother Louise was good, but she had some serious defects that increased the family's poverty.

Her niece Jeanne Vedère confirms: *Louise was a good Christian, sweet, cheerful and industrious. She taught her daughters well. She had everything one could want to be an excellent mother of a family. However, she had one habit that I did not approve of.... From morning till night the women came to the mill. None of them left without having received something to eat.*

She always had wine or bread or cheese when there was nothing else. So she spent more than she received for grinding.

On the other hand, her brother-in-law Dominic Vignes, who was married to Lucila Castérot, Louise's younger sister, explained: *Madame Soubirous drank. She sold her dowry to go drinking. I forbade my wife to see her.* André Sajoux, Louise's nephew, remembers: *She drank. When she had a few cents, she would buy wine, and sometimes she drank too much. She preferred white to red.* But she never made a scandal in the street.

For his part, Father François Soubirous, who was one-eyed in his left eye due to an accident, was a good man, simple and good-humored, incapable of hurting anyone, but he was notoriously careless, not a good businessman, and it was known that he often went to the tavern to play cards. All this contributed to the ruin of the family. Jeanne Vedère testified: *My father used to say that Francis did not know how to be frugal. In his place, he said, I would be better at business. Poor people were in the habit of milling on credit, and then some did not pay, but he did not insist much on being paid. And this, instead of making him*

13

grow in prosperity, led him to utter misery. As for drinking wine, I never saw him in a state of drunkenness.

BERNADETTE

She was the firstborn, born one year after her parents' marriage, on January 7, 1844, in the mill of Boly. Aunt Bernarda, the eldest of the daughters of the widow Castérot, registered her at the town hall as Bernarda Maria (Bernarda by name), but in the parish register she was registered the other way around, as Maria Bernarda (Marie Bernarde). Her godparents at her baptism were her aunt Bernarda Castérot and her cousin Jean-Marie Vedère. She was baptized in the church of St. Pierre de Lourdes, two days after her birth, on January 9, 1844.

When she was ten months old, in November 1844, while her mother was by the fireplace, a line of candles that was burning fell and caught her mother's bodice and set it on fire. Although the burns were not deep, her mother was unable to nurse her. She was also expecting a new baby in February or March. So they had to find a wet nurse.

In the village of Bêrtrès, Marie Aravant (or Marie Laguës) had just lost a two-week-old baby. Louise offered to raise the baby for five francs a month, payable in silver or flour. Aunt Bernarda stayed with the mother for a few days while the child adjusted to the new home. The nurse got used to her and loved her all her life. Sometimes

15

she would go to Lourdes, 5 kilometers away, to see her and bring her a little gift.

She stayed with the nurse for only about ten months and then returned home. She seemed to be in good health until she was ten years old, but soon she began to suffer from asthma, which remained with her for the rest of her life. Bernadette was a loving and happy child with a graceful smile. Being the oldest, she had to take care of her younger siblings and help with the household chores, as they were very poor. When she was ten years old, in 1854, her father could not pay the rent for the mill and they had to move to another mill with a low yield, the Laborde Mill.

When he was eleven years old, a cholera epidemic spread through the Lavadan valleys and claimed many victims. More than thirty people died in Lourdes. Bernadette was attacked by the disease, but she was saved, although her health was very weak. She was smaller than normal and suffered from asthma, but she helped her two younger siblings, Toñita (Antoinette), called Maria at home, and Juan Maria. Both parents had to leave to work elsewhere, and she remained in charge of the household.

On October 23, 1855, grandmother Clara Castérot died and they inherited 900 francs, but they had to move again and rent the mill in Arlizac, 5 kilometers from Lourdes. Dominic Vignes pointed out: *When his mother-in-law Castérot died, he inherited 900 francs, but he did not know how to use it and everything disappeared the same year. Louise's sister, Bernadette, could not bear the chaos, and almost none of the relatives visited them.*

Bernadette rarely went to the school of the Hospice Sisters because she had to take care of her siblings at home. Before the apparitions, Bernadette would say: "I knew only the Our Father, the Hail Mary, the Creed and the invocation: 'O Mary, conceived without sin, pray for us who have recourse to thee.

Nevertheless, she was a happy child. Her nurse Maria Laguës says: *Bernadette, despite the fatigue caused by her asthma, was always cheerful and smiling. She never complained about anything or anybody. She obeyed in everything and never gave a bad answer. She never gave us sadness. She accepted whatever we gave her and was happy.*

As for his parents, they went to Mass every Sunday and prayed the Rosary as a family every evening. They received Communion at Easter. In their home, where everything was lacking, God and daily prayer were not. *There was never a quarrel between Francisco and Luisa, nor a bad word from one to the other, nor from the children to their parents. And they corrected their children severely, but they did not abuse them.*

According to André Sajoux, *Louise loved cleanliness, although she did not get as much of it as she would have liked. Neither she nor the children asked for anything. I never saw them crying because they were hungry. But I often saw Bernadette, Toñita and Juan María, and later Pedro, jumping and having fun on an empty stomach.*

FAMILY POVERTY

Mrs. Estrade says: *One day, about two o'clock in the afternoon, I was praying before the altar of Our Lady in the church at Lourdes, and I thought I was alone, when I noticed that the chairs were moving. I turned around and saw a poorly dressed boy of about six years old. His face was funny, but very pale, which indicated to me that he was a poorly fed child. I went back to my prayers, but the boy continued his task. With a very dry spark I tried to force him to be quiet. The boy obeyed, but in spite of the precautions he took not to make any more noise, he did not succeed. I looked at him more closely and saw that he bent down, scraped the tiles, and immediately put his hand to his mouth. What was he eating? The wax that fell from the candles during a service for the dead. I asked him: "Do you eat wax? He signaled to me, "Are you hungry...would you like to eat something else?*

With repeated nods of his head, he

answered in the affirmative. I immediately left the church with the poor little boy who had become my friend. For a long time, obedient to my invitation, he came to visit me every day as a guest. However, I could never get him to enter the house: he stubbornly remained on the step of the stairs, which he used as a table.

Many months later, I went to visit the Soubirous family because they were talking about Bernadette. There I found my little friend sitting next to Bernadette. I said to him: "Have you also come to see Bernadette? And they both answered me at the same time: "I am her brother. "He is my brother," said Bernadette. It was Juan Maria.

In the winter of 1857, Bernadette was walking through town with her two-year-old brother. The child walked barefoot in clogs. A lady passed by, accompanied by a little girl. It was Irma Jacomet, wife of the Chief of Police, who was walking with her daughter Armanda. Mademoiselle Armande, only five and a half years old, was taking her first lessons in stocking making from the Sisters of the Hospice. With their help, she had just finished her first big project: a pair of little stockings. She had already told her mother: "I want to give her to the poorest child *we can find, even if he is Spanish. As soon as Madame Jacomet had seen little Justin Soubirous, she approached her daughter and spoke into her ear. They had found Armanda's chosen one.*

In 1856, the economic situation of the Soubirous family was worse than ever. They had to leave the mill in Arcizac and were hired as simple day laborers in Lourdes. They rented a small room in the rue du Bourg, but in November they had to leave it and go to live with a second cousin of Louise's, André Sajoux, who lived in the old prison of the city, which had been moved 30 years ago because it was very unhealthy.

André lived on the second floor and gave the Soubirous the basement, called the *prison*, a very dark place where the sun never came. They moved there with the four children they had at the time. They had only a trunk, a suitcase, some chairs and three beds. There was no room for more, as the room was four by five meters.

Bernadette was thirteen years old and could not read, while her sister Toñita was attending school normally, could read, and was preparing for her First Communion. Despite the family's hardships, Bernadette remained a happy child despite her health problems.

The bread they ate was cornbread and was too heavy for Bernadette's stomach. Her mother provided wheat bread and a little sugar and wine for her health. Sometimes her little brothers would take the wheat bread from her before she ate it, but she said nothing because she was like a mother to them.

March 27, 1857, was a bad day for the family. Sergeant Angla arrived at the *jail* with a gendarme looking for two sacks of flour that had been stolen from the baker Maisongrosse, who had accused Father François of having once worked in his bakery. Imagine the sadness of the family without the father at home and with so much poverty.

He was detained for 9 days. On April 4th he was released for lack of evidence. And in the evening, as they did every day, they prayed the Rosary together as a family. Andres Sajoux explained that *he could hear them saying the prayers at night.*

One day, *her uncle, the husband of her godmother Bernadette, returned from Betharram with a number of small rings. They were all too big for Bernadette. She felt sorry for them. Her uncle consoled her by promising to bring her a ring that would fit her finger. The uncle kept his promise and brought her a small ring. But it was so small that she could not wear it. Not to be discouraged, Bernadette made such an effort, using her teeth, that the ring fit with great difficulty. But her finger began to hurt, and soon it was swollen. The swelling and pain increased at the same time. The ring had to be sawed off with a small file, and she laughingly said afterwards: "I never wanted a ring again.*

FALSE DEVOTIONS

In June 1857, the Bishop of Tarbes, Monsignor Laurence, issued a circular against the distortions and the exploitation of the devotion to the Virgin Mary, in order to prevent the faithful from having superstitious ideas about this devotion, since there were pamphlets in circulation that promoted a false cult of Mary. For example, they said: *Virgin Mary, Mother of God, full of grace, whoever carries this prayer will not die of sudden death. Another said: "Virgin Mary, Mother of God, source of consolation, praiseworthy virgin among women". And they added that they had been found wrapped in a cloth from the Holy Sepulchre or that they had been blessed by the Pope. Another said: "The Mother of God, lying on her bed, wept and lamented" .... All those who know this prayer and do not recite it to their neighbors will suffer great grief at the hour of their death.*

CATECHISM STUDY

At the end of June 1857, her nurse took Bernadette into her home in Bartrès, promising to send her to school and catechism classes. In reality, however, she was forced to work hard as a shepherdess tending her flocks of sheep and cows. They did not give her the opportunity to go to school or catechism, except a few times; but in the many hours of solitude in the fields, God spoke to her heart and she learned to talk to Him. She got up early, helped her mistress to dress the children, tidied the house with the maid Jeanne-Marie, and then went to the stable, accompanied by Pigou, the little dog that always accompanied her to the fields. At the foot of a hundred-year-old chestnut tree, she would build a small altar of stones, where she would place a picture of the Virgin Mary and pray a decade of the rosary.

But Bernadette was not happy. She wanted to learn, and one day when a neighbor from Lourdes came to visit her, she gave her this assignment for her parents: "*I am bored here. If you don't mind, go to my parents and tell them to pick me up. I want to go back to Lourdes to take classes and prepare for my First Communion.*

On January 28, 1858, she returned to Lourdes. She was 14 years old. The next day, with her parents' permission, she went to the hospice school run by nuns. She was immediately enrolled and prepared by Father Pomian, who gave catechetical instruction. At that time, she could not read or write, nor could she speak French, only the patois of the region, and she did not know most of the catechism.

FIRST APPEARANCE (February 11)

On February 11, 1858, Bernadette went with her sister Toñita and her friend Juana Abadie to the forest to collect firewood and bones to sell. Juana Abadie explained: *We arrived in front of the grotto. The channel was knee-deep in water.... On the other side of the canal, in the crack in the rock, I saw a bone and in the same place some branches that the water had washed away.*

To get to the cave, we had to cross the bed of the canal. Toñita and Juana threw their clogs on the other side and walked through the water, which was very cold because of the melting snow. Bernadette thought about not following them because the water, which was very cold, could hurt her. On the other hand, she did not want them to go alone. She asked her sister to put some big stones in the water for them to walk over. Toñita wouldn't do it. Then she asked Juana (who was tall and strong) if she could carry her on her shoulders, but she replied: *You can do as we do; if not, stay there.* And Toñita and Juana began to look for bones and firewood and left the place. Bernadette was alone and knew it was twelve o'clock because she had heard the twelve chimes in the church tower. She decided to cross the canal and turned: *I had hardly taken off a stocking when I heard a rumble of wind, like a storm approaching. I turned to look across the meadow and saw that the trees were barely moving. Without stopping my gaze, I caught a glimpse of movement in the branches and blackberry bushes by the side of the cave.*

I continued walking barefoot, and as I was about to put one foot in the water, I heard the same noise in front of me. I raised my eyes and saw a pile of branches and blackberry bushes coming and going in agitation, below the highest opening of the cave, while nothing moved.

Behind the branches, inside the opening, I immediately saw a young woman, all white, not taller than me, who greeted me with a slight bow of her head, while at the same time she held her outstretched arms a little away from her body, her hands open like the holy virgins. A rosary was hanging from her right arm. I was frightened and stepped back. I wanted to call my companions, but I didn't feel up to it. I rubbed my eyes several times, thinking I was deluding myself.

When I raised my eyes, I saw a young girl smiling at me with a very graceful smile that seemed to invite me to approach her. But I was still afraid. But it was not the fear I had felt at other times, because I had always looked at her (Aquéro), *and when you are afraid, you run away immediately.*

Then I had the idea to pray. I put my hand in my pocket, took out my usual rosary, knelt down and tried to make the sign of the cross. But I couldn't bring my hand to my forehead: I dropped it. Meanwhile, the young woman turned on her side and faced me. This time she had the large rosary in her hand. She crossed herself as if to begin to pray. My hand was shaking. I tried to cross myself again and was able to do so. From that moment on, I was no longer afraid.

I prayed with my rosary. The young woman slipped her beads but did not move her lips. As she prayed the rosary, I watched as much as I could. She was wearing a white dress that came down to her feet, only the tips were visible. The dress was closed at the top, around her neck. A white veil, which covered her head, descended over her shoulders and arms to the ground. I saw that she had a yellow rose on each foot. The sash of her dress was blue and fell just below her knees. The rosary chain was yellow, the pearls were white, thick and widely spaced. The young woman was full of life, she was very young and surrounded by light. When I finished the rosary, she greeted me with a smile. She retreated into the cave and suddenly disappeared.

Bernadette said that while she was praying the Our Father and the Hail Marys of the Rosary, the vision did not move her lips. She later clarified that she visibly said the Glorias and bowed her head. Why did she do this? Because the Our Father is the prayer of the needy mortals of this world, and the Hail Mary is the prayer of praise to Mary, and she did not exalt herself. Instead, she prayed the Glorias in honor of the Holy Trinity, bowing her head in gratitude and recognizing that all that she is comes to her from God. On October 24, 1865, Father Cross asked her what color the eyes of the apparition were. She replied: *blue.*

Father Pène asked her to tell him if she had ever seen a lady as beautiful as she was, and she replied: *I have never seen anything so beautiful.* And before he died, when he was already very ill in the monastery infirmary, a five-year-old girl, Madeleine Darfeuille, asked him: *Was she beautiful, he* replied: *Oh yes, so beautiful that when you have seen her once, you want to die to see her again.*

During this first apparition, after the rosary had ended and the vision had disappeared, Bernadette came to her senses while on her knees. At that moment her sister and her friend returned. According to Toñita's testimony: *She was still kneeling and looking into the cave. I called "Bernadette" three times in a row, but she did not answer or turn her head. As I got closer, I threw some pebbles at her. One hit her back, but she didn't move. She was white as if she had died. Suddenly Bernadette came to and looked at us. I said, "What were you doing over there?" "Nothing." "What a fool you are to pray there! But she said, "Prayer is good anywhere. And she crossed the river modestly.*

Bernadette will say: *I was amazed when I went into the water and found it warmer than cold.* And Toñita adds: *Bernadette put on her stockings while sitting on a stone and without being cold. Then she asked us: "Did you see*

anything? "No, and what did you see?".
"Nothing." The friend Juana went home because she was in a hurry. And Toñita adds: *Before we passed the old bridge, she told me: "I saw a lady dressed in white with a blue sash and a yellow rose on each foot.*

When they got home, Toñita told her mother, who thought it was a girl's story and beat her with a stick. Toñita complained and said to Bernadette: *"You are the one who made Mother beat me.* The mother told them that perhaps she was a soul of our ancestors who was in purgatory and that it was necessary to pray for her. When the father found out, he was more direct and scolded Bernadette, thinking that it could be a bad thing. He forbade her to return to the cave.

The next day, Friday, February 12, 1858, Bernadette returned to the hospice school. Many of her friends already knew that something had happened because Jeanne Abadie had told them. They asked her to tell Sister Damiana, who was in the playground at the time. Bernadette excused herself by saying that she did not speak French. *A companion translated her into French, but when what she said was not correct, she corrected it vigorously.*

Sister Damiana advised her not to talk about it again because she might be made fun of. Some of her classmates already called her a liar and Sofia Pailhasson, nine years old, slapped her.

On Saturday, February 13, Bernadette went to confession and told Father Pomian, the parish priest, everything. She told him: *"I saw a white thing in the shape of a lady."* The confessor asked permission to speak to the parish priest about it. The parish priest, who did not know, said solemnly: "We must wait.

SECOND APPEARANCE (February 14)

It was Carnival Sunday, and as she was leaving the church, a dozen of her companions from the hospice surrounded Bernadette, who had already told her sister Toñita that she wanted to go to the grotto, but did not dare ask her mother's permission. So *the companions went to the "jail" to ask their mother's permission, who finally relented and told them to ask their father's permission. Her father, who worked nearby, replied that he would not give her permission, but Mr. Cazenave, for whom she worked, told her: "Let the little girl go. If the one she sees wears the rosary, it's not bad. The father reluctantly agreed. They returned to the house and told her mother.*

Bernadette had some doubts about the vision because she had heard about apparitions of evil spirits and had been told that holy water was a powerful defense against them, that they would disappear when holy water was poured over them. So she took a small bottle and asked her friends to go to church. There she prayed with them and filled the bottle with holy water.

There were about twenty students in all, divided into two groups. Bernadette was in the lead and ran to get there early. When they arrived, they knelt down and began to pray the rosary. At the end of the first ten, Bernadette exclaimed, "Look, the radiance.... Look at her. She has the rosary on her right arm. She is looking at us.

Bernadette stood up and approached the mysterious being and said: <"If you are from God, stay! And she poured holy water on him. She (Aquéro, she would say in her dialect) *smiled, showing that she came from God.* At that moment, Jeanne Abadie, who was behind with the second group of girls, threw a stone from behind to show her displeasure at being late, and it fell on the rock where Bernadette was standing. Bernadette leaned forward with a pale face and stared into the cave, but some of her companions shouted that she was dead. And they said, "Jeanne, you have killed Bernadette. Jeanne did not believe it. She later explained: "Her face lit up. All the girls were crying. I liked them all.

They shook Bernadette, not understanding that she was in ecstasy, and when they saw that she did not respond, they became frightened. Juana ran to tell Bernadette's parents, and others ran to the neighboring Savy Mill to come to their aid. The miller, Mrs. Nicolau, asked her 18-year-old son Antonio for help.

years old and ran to help. In his testimony, Antonio said the following: *They told me:*

35

Bernadette is in the cave of Massabielle. We don't know what she sees. We cannot get her out of there. Come and help us. Without a hat or jacket, I followed my mother and aunt, without begging them, and went down to the cave by a bad and narrow path. When I arrived, I saw three or four poor girls, Toñita Soubirous and Bernadette. She was on her knees, pale, with her eyes extraordinarily open, looking into the cave. Her hands were clasped and the rosary was between her fingers. Tears were streaming from her eyes. She was smiling and her face was beautiful, more beautiful than anything I had ever seen. I felt pain and joy at the same time and throughout the day my heart was moved with emotion and I could not stop thinking about her.

I stayed motionless for a while to look at them. The girls were like me; my mother and my aunt, equally astonished.... Although I saw her smiling, I was worried to see her so pale. Finally, I approached her because my mother told me: "Take her and we will take her home.

I took her by the right arm. She resisted because she wanted to stay. Her eyes kept looking up. She did not complain. But after she put up some resistance, her breathing came in short gasps. I lifted her by one arm and then the other; my mother took her by one of them. As I lifted her up, I dried her eyes and put my hand over them so she couldn't see. I tried to get her to lower her head, but she would raise her head and open her eyes again and smile....

We had a great deal of work getting her up the path; my mother holding one hand and me the other, both pulling her forward, and my aunt and the girls following behind. Without speaking, she did her best to climb back down. It took a lot of strength to pull her down. I alone, though I am quite strong, would have had a hard time getting her to follow me. As we climbed, Bernadette's face remained pale and her eyes, always open, kept looking up. By the time we reached the top, I was sweating. We went down the forest path to the mill, the girl leading us, as before, my mother and I. We were still in the forest, and my mother asked her questions, and so did I. My mother asked her questions and I asked her questions, but she didn't answer us. I felt sad and afraid. Her face and eyes remained the same as before the grotto. He continued to shed tears. From time to time I covered his eyes with my hand and wiped away his tears. He smiled until we reached the mill.

As we entered, at the very threshold, she

37

lowered her eyes and head, and the color returned to her face. We led her into the kitchen and made her sit down. The girls had come with us. When she sat down, I asked her, "What do you see in this hole? Do you see something ugly?" She replied, "Oh no, I see a very beautiful lady. She has a rosary on her arm and her hands are clasped together".

When Bernadette awoke from her ecstasy in Savy's mill, she was surprised because all the time she had been in communication with the vision and praying the rosary with her. A short time later, his mother came with a stick to beat him and scolded him in front of everyone. The miller, seeing that she was going to hit her, shouted at her: *Luisa, why do you want to strike him? Your daughter is an angel from heaven.* Luisa controlled herself and burst into tears. Then she took Bernadette's hand and they both went back to the house.

That carnival Sunday, many people from the surrounding area were in Lourdes and these things were made public. Anthony told what had happened to him and the girls did the same at home. On Carnival Monday, February 15, Bernadette was scorned by the nuns at the hospice school, who told her to stop these carnivals. She was taken to see the superior and told her what she had seen on Sunday. The superior insisted that it was all an illusion and that she should forget everything. On Tuesday the 16th, Mme. Millet's maid went to ask her mother to send Bernadette to tell her what had happened.

How could she refuse in front of Madame Millet, who sometimes gave her work? Madame went to Bernadette's house and got permission to take Bernadette to the grotto very early on Thursday the 18th, with older people like her and Mademoiselle Peyret.

THIRD APPEARANCE (February 18)

On Thursday the 18th, when they came for her at half past five in the morning, Bernadette was still in bed. She got up quickly and they went to Mass together. Madame Millet carried a blessed candle under her cape, and Mademoiselle Peyret carried a sheet of white paper, a pen and an inkwell, with the intention that the apparition would write down her wishes.

Mademoiselle Peyret said that she thought it could be the president of the Daughters of

39

Mary, Elisa Latapie, who had died a month ago. Like the apparition, she wore a blue ribbon around her medal and carried a rosary on the day of the consecration. If she needed prayers, she could write them down.

They arrived at the grotto. They lit the candle (the first to be lit in the grotto before the Virgin) and began to pray the rosary. That day, Bernadette's ecstasy
Bernadette's ecstasy did not make her insensitive to the outside world and was like a bridge between the two worlds. Antoinette Peyret told her: *Ask him what he wants.* Bernadette, inkwell, pen and paper in hand, walked forward until she almost touched the branches of the hanging rose bush. The two companions had risen to follow her, but Bernadette waved them aside. Bernadette rose on tiptoe and held out the paper and pen. She spoke to the apparition, but although she was in incomplete ecstasy, her voice was not audible, although her lips could be seen moving.

He asked: *Madam, would you be so kind as to give me your name in writing?* Aquéro (she) laughed and said: *It is not necessary to write down what I have to say*. (It was the first time I had heard her voice).

Mrs. Millet begged her to ask if they could come back. Bernadette replied that there was nothing to prevent them from returning. Then the vision said to her in her sweetest voice: "Will you do me the favor of coming back here for fifteen days? Bernadette replied, "When I have asked my parents' permission, I will return. "I do not promise to make you happy in this world, but I will make you happy in the next." Having said this, the apparition ascended into the vault and disappeared.

Before leaving the grotto, Bernadette said in Mademoiselle Peyret's ear: *Aquéro* (She) *looked at her smiling.*

Both companions talked about what had happened, and everyone learned that the apparition would come during the next fifteen days, which moved all the people, and many wished to be present.

FOURTH APPEARANCE (February 19)

At school, Bernadette continued to be teased, and some, knowing that she had difficulty memorizing her catechism, would say to her:

"*Tell Our Lady to teach you the catechism.* She endured everything so that she could continue to see the wonderful apparition that made her so happy.

Her parents gave her permission to go to the grotto, and the fortnight of apparitions began, with more and more people coming each day.

Like the day before, Bernadette went to Mass early with Mrs. Millet. She was accompanied by her aunt Bernadette. In the grotto, Bernadette had a lighted candle in her Bernadette had a lighted candle in her left hand and her rosary in her right hand. At the third Hail Mary, the apparition appeared. After a few greetings and smiles, Bernadette's face was so beautiful that one wanted to cry just to see her. Sometimes she would turn white like a candle and people thought she was dying. Her mother, who was also there, said: "*My God, I beg you not to take my daughter away from me.*

The vision ended after half an hour. Bernadette said that at one point of the apparition, unexpectedly, as if vomited from the Gave, howling could be heard that disturbed the silence of Massabielle. And a rabid voice, dominating the other voices, shouted: *Run away, run away.* She realized that the cries were not only directed at her, but also at the vision, who was looking in that direction and, with sovereign authority, silenced the crowd of demons.

Returning from the grotto, he went to the house of his Aunt Basilia, with whom he had arranged to go early the next day to avoid the crowds.

FIFTH APPEARANCE (February 20)

Despite the winter cold, she arrived at the grotto with Aunt Basilia at six o'clock in the morning on Saturday, February 20, when very few people were there. *When he arrived, he took the blessed candle in his left hand and the rosary in his right. The vision was not long in coming, and all the people felt that they were seeing her, for she was concentrated in the grotto with her face up and smiling. Her own mother, surprised, moved and amazed, said: "I did not recognize my daughter.*

On the way home, she confided that the Blessed Mother had taught her, word for word, a prayer just for her that she would pray every day of her life. Twenty years later she would say: "I pray it every day. No one outside of me knows.

SIXTH APPEARANCE (February 21)

When she arrived at the grotto that Sunday, accompanied by her mother and her aunt Bernarda, a huge crowd was waiting for her. On that day, there were three gendarmes to keep order. There was also a well-known person in Lourdes, Doctor Dozous, who did not believe in such things and went to investigate, carefully observing Bernadette's every move. He says: *I wanted to know the condition of his*

of his circulation and respiration. I took one of his arms and placed my fingers over the radial artery. The pulse was steady and regular. Breathing was easy. There was nothing to indicate nervous excitement.

Therefore, she will conclude: *Bernadette is not affected by catalepsy. This disease robs those who suffer from it of voluntary movement. And Bernadette can move at will. I saw her, when she was in ecstasy, put her hand near the flame of the lighted candle to prevent the wind from extinguishing it.*

After the apparition, Bernadette attended high mass. As the girls were leaving the church, an employee of the mayor's office called her. The Imperial Procurator, Dr. Dutour, wanted to speak with her. She went quietly. The Procurator kept her standing throughout the audience, trying to intimidate her so that she would not return to the grotto and thus avoid possible social problems. He said to her:

- *Do you intend to go to the grotto every morning?*
- *Yes, sir. I promised to go for two weeks.*

- *But didn't the director of the hospice and the guard sister, who are very pious women, tell you that there is no need to go back, that the vision you have is a dream, an illusion? Why don't you follow their advice? That would prevent them from taking care of you.*

- *I feel such satisfaction when I go to the grotto!*
- *You could abstain... and you could be forbidden.*
- *I feel drawn by an irresistible force.*

- *But beware! There are many people who assume that you and your parents are trying to take advantage of people's gullibility. I can assume that myself. Your family is very poor. Since your visits to the cave, they have bestowed upon you favors that you could not even dream of, and now you may be expecting greater ones. I must say that if you are not sincere in your testimony about the apparitions, or if you and your parents profit from them, you will be persecuted and severely punished.*

- *I do not expect to profit in this life.*

- *You say so. But haven't you already accepted Mrs. Millet's hospitality? Don't your parents hope to improve their situation with you and your visions, even if they are only dreams, or perhaps lies, which would be much worse?*

- *Mrs. Millet wanted me in her house. She came looking for me. I went with her at her request. I never worried about myself. I never lied to her or anyone else.*

That night, Bernadette cried because she was causing her parents so much trouble, because the police were watching her and threatening her if she returned to the cave. Her father, who was called to the police station, assured the commissioner that his daughter would never go there again. But Bernadette had promised to go for two weeks. Would she have the strength to resist Massabielle's attraction? Would she have to disobey her parents? Would she have to miss Madame's appointment? Her head was spinning, not understanding anything and not knowing what would happen.

MONDAY, FEBRUARY 22

It was a day of disappointment. First, she was not allowed to go to Mass or to the grotto. When the time came, she meekly went to the hospice school. The policeman in charge of guarding the grotto returned without incident. In the afternoon, Bernadette tells Mademoiselle Estrade, who has come to visit her at home: *I cannot move my legs, except to go to Massabielle.* And without permission, as if on the run, she went with Mademoiselle Estrade. Two policemen saw them and accompanied them. A large number of people also ran and came to meet Madame.

But the Lady did not appear that day, and Bernadette was very sad because she thought it was her fault. Some people, also disappointed, thought that the apparitions were over. Others encouraged her, saying, "*She will come tomorrow morning. She must have waited for you in the morning, as on other days.* Some hinted: *The lady is afraid of the gendarmes.*

On her return, her aunts sent her to rest at Savy's mill, where her mother came to meet her.

Miss Estrade stated that she was sitting beside him when his mother arrived. She says: <I did not know it was her mother. This poor woman was pale, and from time to time she looked at the little girl with concern. I asked her if she knew the little girl.

- *Oh, Miss. I am his unhappy mother.*

- *Unhappy? Why?*

- *You can see very well what is happening to us. We are threatened with imprisonment. Some laugh at us, others feel sorry for us and say that Bernadette is sick.*

- *What do you think?*
- *The child is not a liar. I believe she is not capable of deceiving us. She is not ill. I have*

forbidden her to return to the cave, and yet she has returned. However, she is not disobedient; she has assured me that she is driven by a force that she cannot explain.

In the evening her parents discussed the matter and thought that if she was driven by a higher power, it was useless to forbid her. The fact that the Lady did not manifest herself, they thought, was her fault. Maybe they were fighting Heaven. And they agreed that she could go if she felt the call.

SEVENTH APPEARANCE (February 23)

Early on Tuesday morning, February 23, Bernadette went to the cave. There she met Dr. Dozous, the captain of the castle, Mr. Laffitte, the military intendant, the lawyer Dufo and Mr. Estrade, the tax collector, and many others. Mr. Jean-Baptiste Estrade, an exceptional witness, who went there to mock and laugh, reports: *Bernadette went down on her knees, took her rosary from her pocket and saluted deeply. She made all her movements effortlessly, naturally, just as the little girl would have done in the parish church during her ordinary prayers. As the first beads of the rosary slipped through her fingers, she glanced at the rock inquiringly, showing the impatience of her waiting.*

Suddenly, as if struck by lightning, she had a flash of admiration and seemed to be born to a new life. Her eyes brightened and sparkled; a seraphic smile formed on her lips; an indefinable grace spread over her. In the narrow prison of her flesh, the soul of the visionary seemed to strive to manifest itself and express its joy.
Bernadette was no longer Bernadette!

Spontaneously, all the men present took off their hats and bowed like the humblest of women. The hour of
The hour of discussion had passed and, like all those who witnessed this scene in heaven, we turned our eyes from the ecstatic to the rock and from the rock to the ecstatic. We saw nothing, we heard nothing, but what we could see and understand was that a conversation had begun between the mysterious "Lady" and the girl in front of us.

After these first transports caused by the arrival of the Lady, the visionary assumed the attitude of a person listening. Her gestures, her physiognomy, perfectly demonstrated all the phases of a conversation.

Sometimes smiling, sometimes serious, Bernadette nodded her head in agreement or seemed to ask a question herself. When "Madame" spoke, the child trembled with joy; when, on the contrary, she addressed her petitions to her, she was humbled and moved to tears.

At certain moments, one could sense that the conversation was interrupted; then the girl would return to praying the Rosary, but without taking her eyes off the rock: it was as if she did not want to close them for fear that the marvelous object of her contemplation would disappear from her sight.

The ecstatic usually ended her prayers with a greeting to the hidden "Lady". I, who have perhaps lived too much in the world and found in it models of grace and distinction, have never seen anyone who greeted with the grace and distinction of Bernadette.

During the ecstasy, the girl crossed herself at intervals. That same day, on my way back to the grotto, I said that if they crossed themselves in heaven, they could not do it any other way.

The ecstasy continued for about an hour. Toward the end, the visionary, on her knees, moved from the place of her prayers to almost under the rose bush hanging from the rock. There, as if in a fervent act of adoration, she gathered herself, kissed the ground and, still on her knees, returned to the place from which she had begun. His face lit up with a new radiance; then, gradually, without any jolt, almost imperceptibly, the rapture faded until it disappeared.

The visionary continued to pray for a few moments, but then we had only the sweet but rustic face of the little daughter of the Soubirous family. Finally, Bernadette stood up, joined her mother and disappeared into the crowd. ....

Even though the Lady of the Rock wished to remain invisible, I felt her presence and was convinced that her motherly gaze had stopped above my head. Oh, the most solemn hour of my life! I was thrilled to the point of delirium at the thought that I, a scoffing and vain man, had been permitted to occupy a place near the Queen.

EIGHTH APPEARANCE (February 24)

On Wednesday, February 24, 400 to 500 people were gathered in the grotto, according to the report that the sergeant of Lourdes sent to his superior. Our Lady appeared before the end of the first decade of the rosary. After five or six minutes, Bernadette came out of ecstasy, stood up, wept and said:

Who touched the bush? <That is what she called the wild rose bush that had moved because a young girl, who wanted to see the visionary better, had pushed it aside. For Bernadette, it was the branch where the Lady's feet rested and where the yellow roses were. Therefore, it was disrespectful to the Lady to touch it. After the wake-up call, she went to the vault of the grotto. His face looked very sad.

And he repeated with trembling lips: Repent, repent, repent. Everyone heard and repeated the same words. The *Lady* addressed the message to everyone: *Do penance for the salvation of sinners.*

NINTH APPEARANCE (February 25)

On Thursday, February 25, Bernadette went to the cave before dawn. She went with flashlights. About 400 people were waiting. Shortly after arriving, the *Lady* appeared. Almost immediately, Bernadette began to walk on her knees. As she reached the entrance to the cave, she gently pushed aside the overhanging branches coming down from the rock without pausing.... When she reached the bottom of the cave, still on her knees, she turned around. Everyone was watching her movements intently. After finding nothing in the cave, she went to the Gave River. She later explained: "*The lady* said to me, '*Go and drink at the well and wash yourself.*' *Not finding the well, I went to drink at the Gave. She told me it was not there. She showed me with her finger where the well was. I went there. I found only a little dirty water; I put my hand in it, but I could not drink it; I dug and the water came out murkier. Three times I threw it away and the fourth time I could drink it.*

Everyone saw Bernadette with a dirty face and many had a negative feeling and said: *She's crazy, she's crazy*. Aunt Bernadette quickly wiped her mouth and chin. The people's disappointment reached its peak when they saw her, still on her knees, take three handfuls of grass and put it in her mouth. It was a kind of dorina, like a very green clover. The *Lady* had just commanded him: "*Go and eat of the grass that you will find there.*

said one of her catechism classmates, Vicenta Garros: *I saw Bernadette, at the command of the apparition, cut the root of the plant she held in her hands and make an effort to eat some leaves, chewing them for a while and spitting them out, because, as she told me, the herb was very hard and bad.*

When the apparition was over, Bernadette and her aunt left in a hurry to escape the crowd, who were disappointed, thinking that she had acted out a comedy. But in reality, the *Lady had wanted to teach her to put into practice what she had told her in the previous apparition: penance. And also to teach him obedience and humility to accept what she told him.*

The people left disappointed, not realizing that where Bernadette had drunk the water, there were already the first gushes of the miraculous water that would bring health to thousands and thousands of sick people in the following years and centuries.

FRIDAY, FEBRUARY 26

On that day, the Lady did not come to the appointment, but all those present were surprised to see that in the place where Bernadette had dug the day before, there was a ribbon of water that they had never seen before. This ribbon of water was growing by the minute. Everyone was excited about it. But the visionary was heartbroken, thinking that she might be to blame for the *Lady's* absence. And after devoutly reciting the rosary with those present, she sadly retired to the arms of her mother and godmother. The *Lady* , however, wished to make up for her absence on February 22 and 26 by making two more appearances outside of the fortnight. They will be on March 25th and April 5th.

TENTH APPEARANCE (February 27)

On Saturday morning, February 27, it was freezing cold, but the crowd had grown. On that day, Bernadette was seen smiling and sometimes turning pale, but also kissing the ground several times as an act of penance and humility, as the *Lady* had told her: *Kiss the ground in penance for sinners.*

Sister Peyrard, who was a Sister of Charity of St. Vincent de Paul, said: "*After praying one or two decades of the Rosary, Bernadette saw the apparition, which we could see by the change in her face. From the first moments, Bernadette greeted the invisible Lady in three stages: one with a slight bow, the second with a greater bow, and the third almost to the ground. She was radiant with joy and expressed her happiness with little bursts of childish laughter. I had never seen her so happy. You could tell that she was talking to the apparition, and suddenly she began to climb up to the grotto on her knees, kissing the earth several times. When she reached the grotto, she stopped and put a finger to her lips* (to indicate silence) *and, extending her arms with an energetic sign, motioned for all to bow, but most remained motionless as they were. Again he made the same sign with great force. And they all bowed down and kissed the ground. We later learned that it was an act of penance that the apparition asked her to do for sinners.*

After the ecstasy, Bernadette went to the miraculous well and drank several times, washed her face and picked several blades of grass. When she returned home, she confided to her aunt what the Lady had told her: *You will tell the priests to build a chapel here.*

In the afternoon, she and her aunt went to the parish house to talk to the parish priest, Father Peyramale. He was a stout man, with a broad uncovered forehead, with a grave and imposing manner. He was a good mountain man, but his corpulence was intimidating and many people were afraid of him. He had forbidden his three vicars to go to the grotto and did not believe in such things. The Bishop of Tarbes, Monsignor Laurence, laughed at the alleged apparitions, according to the negative report that Father Peyramale had sent him. The priest asked Bernadette a few questions, but she did not want to give any importance to his words, since she did not know who this *lady* was, nor what her name was. Nevertheless, he insisted that if the *Lady* thought she had the right to ask him to build a chapel, she should tell him who she was and immediately make the rose bush in the grotto bloom.

ELEVENTH APPEARANCE (February 28)

On Sunday, February 28, it rained until late at night. The most remarkable thing about this apparition was that Bernadette was more penitent than ever. She tried to walk on her knees, but she almost couldn't because there were about 2,000 people. Two policemen had to make way for her. She went up a distance of seven or eight meters and then down to her usual place. And he went up again up to three times, as the *lady* indicated, as an act of penance. Sometimes she slipped because the ground was very muddy, but neither her clothes nor she was soiled. But when she kissed the ground, she soiled her lips and hands. When he saw her kissing the floor, the sworn guard, Pedro Callet, shouted: *Everybody kiss the ground.* And everyone obeyed. Those who could knelt down and kissed the ground repeatedly. The vast majority could not reach the ground because of the large number of people, but they tried to obey as much as possible. It was still raining and some were shouting: *Close your umbrellas.* And they all closed them.

Bernadette gave the parish priest's order to the lady to say her name and make the rose bush bloom. When she returned, she went to the parish house to tell the priest that she had fulfilled his mission, but the *lady* had only smiled.

That same day, the examining magistrate called Bernadette in for questioning. The security guard, Leon Latapie, wrote down the account of the interrogation and wrote: "After the high mass, the commissioner came to meet me in front of the church and said to me: 'Stay here with me for a while. When the sisters came out of the hospice with their little students, the commissioner said to me, "Do you know Bernadette?" "Yes." "Stop her when she comes out."

When she came out next to the sister, lined up like all the others, I gently took her arm. "Why are you stopping her?" the sister asked me, bursting into tears. "I have this order." Bernadette asked, "What do you want?" I replied, "Little girl, you must come with us." She burst out laughing and said, "Hold me, or I will run away. I was next to the little one, and the commissary was behind both of us. People watched us without saying a word, admiring us.

We went to the house of Mr. Rives, the examining magistrate, who was staying with the notary, Mr. Claverie. When we entered, the judge said to Bernadette in dialect:

- Already here, tunantuela?
- Yes, sir, I am here.
- Let's lock you up... What are you looking for in the grotto? Why are you driving so

60

many people crazy? Somebody is driving you to do this. We'll put you in jail.

- I am willing. Lock me in, but make it solid and tight, otherwise I'll run away.

The gentlemen did not laugh. The judge said:

- You must renounce returning to the cave.
- I will not deprive myself of going there.
- You will be locked up.
- If I can't, I won't go.
- I will let you die in prison.

At that moment, the Sister Superior of the hospice came in. She was crying. She said: "I beg you gentlemen to release the child; do not let her die.

Bernadette had to be a saint or have a lot of inspiration from heaven to keep her blood cold. The judge said to the commissioner:

What are we going to do with her? Let her

go: there is nothing to do with her.

Bernadette sat in front of the judge, the

judge at his table, Mr. Jacomet.

Jacomet, and I stood next to Bernadette.

As she was leaving with the Sister, Bernadette said to her, "I want to go back; it will be the last Thursday.

TWELFTH APPEARANCE (March 1)

On Monday, March 1, at seven o'clock in the morning, Bernadette was in the cave again. This time she was accompanied by her mother and her father, who went to protect her from so many people. It was on this day that a cassock was seen for the first time. Father Dézirat, 27 years old, who lived at that time with his parents in Barbazan-Debat, was present.

According to the calculations of the police commissioner, there were 1,300 people, but there were many others who arrived by other routes and were not counted. There were people from all walks of life: workers, peasants, citizens, soldiers. .... The priest Dézirat explained: *I was a meter away from Bernadette. In her posture and in the features of her face, one could see that her soul was happy. What deep peace! What serenity! What high contemplation! Her smile was beyond comparison..... The girl's look at the apparition was no less enchanting than her smile. It is impossible to imagine anything so pure, so gentle, so kind.....*

When Bernadette came out of her ecstasy, I watched her carefully. What a difference between what I saw then and what I had seen at the moment of the apparition! There is the same difference between matter and spirit. The crowd experienced a sweet awe: only Bernadette saw the apparition, but everyone felt her presence. Joy, mingled with fear, was on everyone's face. It is impossible to imagine a more pious spectacle. Oh, how good it was there! It seemed to me that I was at the gates of paradise.

Something strange happened that day. Juan Bautista Estrade says: At *one point the little girl lifted the rosary as high as her arms would allow and held it up for almost a minute. Then she put it in her pocket. She took out another, waved it, and held it up in the same way as the first. He saluted, smiled and prayed again. The people took out their rosaries, waved them, and shouted*

"Hail Mary". Then they knelt down with tears in their eyes. The enemies of the apparitions spread the rumor that the little girl had blessed the rosaries.

What had happened? Mrs. Pauline Sans had given her rosary to Bernadette and asked her, since she could not go to the grotto for health reasons, to use her own rosary to pray. Bernadette said: <"I promised to please her and I did. Towards the end of the apparition, the "Lady" asked me where my rosary was and I replied that it was in my pocket. She said: "Show it to me. I put my hand in my pocket and showed it to her, holding it in the air for a while. The "lady" said to me: "Use this one. And I did it right away.

Father Pène asked her: *Is it true that you blessed the rosaries in the grotto this morning?* And she answered with a smile: *Women do not wear a stole* (implying that they are not priests to bless). Let us note that the *lady* preferred that he use her rosary of a few cents instead of Madame Pauline's, which was very beautiful and more expensive.

On that day, March 1, the first miraculous

healing took place. *In the middle of the night, 38-year-old Catherine Latapie, known as Chouat, set out for Lourdes. She was nine months pregnant. She took her two youngest children with her. The cave was 7 kilometers away. An instinctive impulse had set her on her way, as if pulling her from the bottom of an abyss. In October 1856, she had climbed an oak tree to shake acorns for her pigs and fallen. The doctor was able to set her dislocated arm, but two of her fingers were twisted and paralyzed. It was her right hand. And Catherine could not spin or knit or do anything useful.*

Catherine watched the apparition with her two little ones; then she climbed to the bottom of the grotto, to the source of the little stream. She put her hand in it and a great gentleness came over her. The shrunken fingers had suddenly regained their agility....

A sharp pain in his heart cut short his thanks. And she murmured: "Holy Virgin, you who have just healed me, allow me to return home!

He quickly took his children by the hand. She walked the seven kilometers back to Loubajac without stopping. As soon as she arrived, she gave birth without any help and "almost without pain. The midwife, hastily alerted, did not arrive until she heard the first cry of the newborn. It was a boy: John the Baptist, who became a priest and was called the miracle child.

THIRTEENTH APPEARANCE (March 2)

Nothing special happened on Tuesday, March 2, but after the apparition, Bernadette went to the parish house to give a message to the pastor. She went with her aunt, Basilia Casterot, who explained: *"I went with her because the apparition had told her that I wanted a procession. The parish priest replied: "How, liar, do you expect us to make a procession to this "Lady"? He walked around the room full of anger and said: "It is a disgrace to have a family like this that makes trouble in the city and does nothing but make people run away. We will do something better: We will give you a torch and you will go to the procession alone, you don't need priests. You don't need priests. You don't see anything, a lady can't come out of a hole". But when the priest changed things, Bernadette told him: "I didn't tell you that, Father. He would say: "You are sick. And he would repeat, "Ask him his name. "I, she would say, would ask him, and he would smile. The priest would come and go, shouting around the*

room: *"Come on, come on, a lady, a procession."*
It was frightening to see and hear.

The scene ended by telling us: *You may leave. Let her go to school. Don't let her go to the grotto anymore. Let's get this over with!*[43] .

As Bernadette left the rectory, she felt uneasy because he had not told her the whole message. And they had to return in the afternoon, despite their fears, to tell the priest that the *Lady* also wanted a chapel to be built.

FOURTEENTH APPEARANCE (March 3)

On Wednesday, March 3, at dawn, Bernadette arrived at the grotto accompanied by her mother. They both prayed for a while. Then, both sobbing, they got up and walked away in deathly silence. There were three thousand people there, and the apparition had not appeared, which left the girl full of sadness.

At half past nine in the morning, her cousin, Andres Sajoux, came to comfort her and told her that if she wanted, he would accompany her again. She felt the call and accepted. In the afternoon, they walked along the road below the castle so as not to go through the town and so that no one would see them. There were people, but not many. The *lady* introduced herself and said to him: *In the morning you did not see me because there were some people who wanted to see your behavior in my presence and they were not worthy. They stayed in the cave overnight and defiled it.*

After the apparition, Bernadette went back to the parish priest and told him: "The Lady smiled when I told her that you asked her to work a miracle. I told her to make the rose bush bloom. She smiled again, but she wants a chapel. The priest replied, "Do you have the money to build it? "No, Father. "Neither do I, so tell Our Lady to give it to you.

FIFTEENTH APPEARANCE (March 4)

Thursday, March 4, was the last of the fifteen days promised by the apparition. On that day, the people were expecting a great miracle and, according to Sergeant Angla, there would be about 20,000 people. Bernadette arrived, preceded by two policemen who led the way to the usual place. She was accompanied by her mother and some members of her family. Holding the lighted candle in her left hand and the rosary in her right, she prayed continuously until the third Hail Mary of the second decade. At that moment, her face changed wonderfully and everyone exclaimed: *Now he sees her*. They all fell to their knees. Before the apparition, she continued to pray the rosary. When she finished the rosary, she brought the fingers on which she was holding the crucifix to her forehead three times in a row without success. The third time she made a beautiful sign of the cross. When asked afterwards why she had not been able to make the sign of the cross, she said it was because Our Lady had slipped the rosary through her fingers and she had made the sign of the cross. It was the longest ecstasy of the last fifteen days.

In the apparition of March 4, Bernadette prayed three complete Rosaries during the ecstasy. It seems that the apparition wanted to show that she was Our Lady of the Rosary and thus recommend this devotion to the Christian people. The parish priest had asked for the rose bush to bloom, and Mary made the rose bush of St. Dominic bloom, that is, the Rosary of Our Lady, since the Rosary is a place of roses.

Police Commissioner Jacomet, in his report

to his superiors, considered it a miracle that there was not the slightest incident and reported 34 smiles and 24 greetings in the grotto. At the end of the vision, Bernadette withdrew. The people were disappointed because they had waited in vain for a miracle, but no one asked her any questions. Nevertheless, many of these people went to her house to talk to her.

People passed through the Soubirous home for two hours, entering through one door and leaving through another. Most wanted to greet Bernadette. Some just shook her hand, others gave her a hug or a kiss. Sergeant Angla explained: *We had to put two gendarmes to guard the house and keep the fanatics at a distance. Those who had rosaries approached Bernadette to have them touched. This ceremony was long. But I did not find that either the Soubirous or Bernadette accepted money, and I know that money was offered to them, but she never accepted it.*

Mr. Martin Tarbès stated that *while he was waiting to go in to see Bernadette at her house, a gendarme asked those who came out if they had given him money. They all replied that they had not*[47].

In the afternoon, Bernadette returned to the rectory to remind the pastor of the messages to make a procession to the grotto and build a chapel there. The priest again insisted that if she returned, as many believed it would be the last apparition, he would ask her name.

SIXTEENTH APPEARANCE (March 25)

Thursday, March 25, was the feast of the Annunciation. From the fourth day, Bernadette continued her normal life, attending school and preparing for her First Communion. However, her parents and the nuns who knew her noticed a profound change in the way she prayed the rosary and made the sign of the cross. She prayed a lot and did some penance for the conversion of sinners, especially when she had to endure the questions of pilgrims.

There was also a noticeable change among the people. On March 15, the parish priest reported to the bishop that he had noticed a much larger than usual attendance at the weekly talks. Soon there was talk of miraculous healings. A fifteen-year-old boy had gone to the grotto, washed his very sick eyes with water from the fountain, and was cured. In the Pique family, a

12-year-old boy, very sick, went to drink the water of the grotto and a great improvement was observed. Twenty years earlier, Louis Bouriette had lost the sight in his right eye due to the explosion of a drill. He rubbed his eye with the water his daughter had brought from the grotto's well, and he was cured. And so on and so forth, other cases that amazed the people who continued to go to the grotto as a place of pilgrimage.

On the night of March 24-25, Bernadette awoke and felt in her heart the call of the *Lady*. With her parents' permission, she left at five o'clock in the morning. When she arrived at the place, the soft light was already shining under the rose bush, as if it had been waiting for her. The apparition had come early.

The "Lady," said Bernadette, *was gentle, smiling, and looked at the crowd as a loving mother looks at her children. As I knelt before her, I asked her forgiveness for being late. She, who was always so kind to me, nodded to me, indicating that I had no need to apologize. Then I expressed to her all my affection and the happiness I felt to see her again. After telling her all that my heart was telling me, I took the rosary.*

At that moment, Bernadette felt the desire to know her name. The vision moved under the rose bush and rose from the ground, stopping under the source of the vault. Bernadette rose and approached it. Her parents and some friends followed and surrounded her. And then she asked her: *"Madam," would you please tell me who you are?* But she replied with a smile.

The second time he asks her, and again another smile. She will say: *I don't know why, but I felt braver and asked her again for the favor of telling me her name.*

Then the apparition, who had remained with joined hands, opened her arms, bent them as in the miraculous medal, let the rosary slide down to her wrist, joined her hands again, placed them on her breast as if to stop the beating of her heart, raised her eyes to heaven and said her secret: *I am the Immaculate Conception.* Then the apparition smiled again, stopped speaking, and disappeared smiling.

A friend of the family, Mrs. Filias-Nicolau, asked Bernadette:

Why are you so happy? And she answered: *For she said unto me: "I am the Immaculate*

Conception". A classmate, Jeanne-Marie Tourré, said that on the *way home she repeated many times: "I am the Immaculate Conception." And she asked him, "What are you repeating? And she replied, "I am repeating the name of the Lady so that I will not forget it.*

When Bernadette got home, all she could think about was going to the parish priest to tell him the good news. She went there almost immediately. The good priest Peyramale, on hearing the lady's name, asked her if she knew what it meant. She replied that she did not. He told her:

- *How can you say what you don't understand?*
- *From the grotto to here, I have not stopped repeating these words.*

But the priest was very moved. He went to the tent of Mrs. Maria Ida Ribettes and said to her*: The Lady said to him: "I am the Immaculate Conception. I was so moved that I almost fell down.*

When it was explained to Bernadette that the Immaculate Conception was none other than the Virgin Mary, she was filled with happiness for such a good Mother, whom she had loved so much since her childhood and to whom she had prayed so often at the picture in the parish church and also when she was a shepherdess in the country.

The Virgin Mary wanted to sign the Bull *Ineffabilis Deus* of December 8, 1854, in which Pope Pius IX declared the Immaculate Conception of the Virgin Mary to be a dogma of faith. It thus confirmed the authority of the Pope. When Bernadette wrote a letter to Pope Pius IX on December 17, 1876, she remarked: "I have often said to myself: How good the Blessed Virgin is! One could say that she came to confirm the word of our Holy Father.

But from the beginning there were some theologians who said that the Virgin Mary could not have said, *I am the Immaculate Conception*, because it was theologically incorrect. She should have said: *I am the Virgin of the Immaculate Conception.* But Jesus also said: *I am the way, the truth and the life; I am the light of the world; I am the resurrection and the life.* In this case, a personal quality is taken for the whole person. It is not that Jesus is only light and nothing else, or that he is a way. The same can be said of Mary. An outstanding quality of her person, such as her

Immaculate Conception, is said for the whole person, as if she were saying: *I am she who was conceived immaculate* (to conceive the Immaculate in my womb). Let us not forget that these words were spoken on the day when the feast of the Annunciation was celebrated, that is, the conception or incarnation of Jesus in the womb of Mary. Here we see the union between the conception of Mary and the conception of Jesus, between the Immaculate and the Immaculate, between Mary and Jesus, forever. This union is manifested permanently and in a special way at the moment of the consecration of the Mass, when the priest, or rather Jesus through the priest, says those words to be re-conceived in bread and wine by Mary, who is always present at the Mass to assist the new birth of Jesus in the Eucharist. At this moment Jesus could say: *I am the Eucharist; and Mary: I am the Mother of the Eucharist.*

Pope John Paul II says in the encyclical *Ecclesia de Eucharistia* No. 57:
Just as the Church and the Eucharist are an inseparable binomial, so too is the binomial Mary and the Eucharist. For this reason, the recollection of Mary in the Eucharistic celebration has been unanimous since ancient times in the Churches of the East and West.

On the other hand, we should not forget that Pope Pius IX had defined the Immaculate Conception of Mary as a dogma of faith on December 8, 1854, four years earlier. Therefore, we can say that Mary wanted to unite the binomial Jesus and Mary with the Pope and confirm his authority by declaring her Immaculate Conception four years after the dogmatic definition. And perhaps she was thinking of exalting the authority of the Pope who, in 1870, would define papal infallibility in the First Vatican Council.

After the apparition of March 25, when Our Lady spoke her name, Father Peyramale had a more positive attitude toward Bernadette and defended her against some people and authorities who were against her. He even managed to get Bernadette to continue her studies at the free boarding school after making her First Communion. She also managed to get her family to move from the *prison* slum to a better house.

The parish priest helped Bernadette's father without giving him any money. The bishop of Tarbes bought the mill in Savy, where Bernadette was born, and rented it to her father. In this way, he was helped in the business he wanted to do to support the family. As the parish priest said to the bishop: "*He has become your tenant. And I have assured him that Your Excellency will never forget him and will always help him.*

However, the parish priest did not want to commit himself completely and waited for the opinion of the investigating commission appointed on July 28, 1858, before giving his own. He asked God for a clear sign to believe. And God gave it to him. He says: *One day, while giving communion, I saw a person who had a luminous halo around his head. This vision surprised me. I gave her communion without knowing who it was, but I followed her with my eyes until she reached her place, and when she bent down to kneel, I recognized Bernadette Soubirous. From that moment on, my worries were over and I no longer doubted the apparitions.*

REFUSAL OF HANDOUTS

Many people approached Bernadette to ask her about the apparitions. And with good will and sincerity, they wanted to help her financially, to help her when they saw her poverty, but she never accepted anything, neither she nor her family. Her mother said clearly: *We would live comfortably if my daughter had wanted to accept the money that was offered to her; sometimes insistently.*

Bernadette was incorruptible in this matter of charity, but her brothers were more condescending. One day, a lady gave Toñita a two-franc coin. Bernadette saw it and said with authority: *No, no, no money.*

Another day, her brother Jean-Marie came home with two francs, saying that some gentlemen had given them to him for accompanying them to the cave to fetch water from the spring. When Bernadette heard this, she slapped him and ordered him to return the two francs. He obeyed, and when he returned, Bernadette searched him to make sure he had not hidden them.

A visitor, Rafaello Ginnasi, the Pope's nephew, offered her a rosary of great value, blessed by the Pope, and asked Bernadette to accept it as a gift and to give him the rosary she held in her hands during the apparitions. But she did not accept. *Rafaello's repeated insistence clashed with Bernadette's firmness.*

Madame de Court from Lyon came to see Bernadette and tried to help her out of her poverty. But she could not get her to accept any gift and decided to use part of her fortune to decorate the places where the Virgin Mary had appeared.

Dr. Dozous writes *Many people who visited Bernadette and her family in my presence one day were saddened to see their detachment and asked me to beg them to accept their gifts of money because they would be happy. Several bags of money were placed on the table with the request to accept them. But they met the same fate as so many others who had given money to the Soubirous family.*

Another day, some rich people gave money to the priest to buy white bread for the Soubirous family. It was a vain ruse. The first loaf of 12 pounds was returned intact, and the parish priest had to return the money to the donors. And so on and so forth. Nevertheless, the parish priest accepted the alms left in the grotto for the poor and gave them to the Charity Fund. Later, these funds were used to build the chapel.

SEVENTEENTH APPEARANCE (April 7)

The pilgrimages to the grotto continued uninterrupted. On April 4, Easter Day, 3,625 pilgrims arrived, according to Mr. Jacomet, the police commissioner. The next day, 5,445. The devotees placed a plaster image in the hollow of the rock of the grotto to perpetuate her memory. On Easter Wednesday, April 7, at six o'clock in the morning, Bernadette went to the grotto. According to the commissary's report, there were about 1,200 people there in silent prayer. The Blessed Mother appeared to her again for about three-quarters of an hour. Doctor Dozous was there. Bernadette held a lighted candle. *When the Virgin Mary appeared,* according to Julia Garros, *the candle slipped little by little until it reached the ground and the flame remained in her hand.*

Some of those present, realizing this, cried

out: "*My God, it's burning*. But Dr. Dozous responded with authority: *Let her go!* So he remained with his hand in the flames for several minutes, without Bernadette making any sign of pain. When the ecstasy was over, the candle fell. Dr. Dozous took Bernadette's hand, rubbed it with his right elbow and said forcefully: *There is nothing!* These words caused great excitement in the crowd.

The doctor took possession of the candle, rekindled it, and cunningly placed it several times under Bernadette's screaming left hand:
It burns me!

Dr. Dozous himself wrote: *She was on her knees praying with great fervor the prayers of the Rosary, which she held in her left hand, while in her right hand she held a large, blessed, lighted candle. As she began to ascend on her knees toward the grotto, her right hand came up to her left hand and placed the flame of the candle under the fingers of that* (left) *hand. The fingers were separated so that the flame could easily pass between them. As the flame was activated at that moment by a rather strong gust of air, it seemed to me that it did not produce any change on his skin. Astonished at this strange fact, I prevented some people from removing the candle and, taking my watch, I observed the fact for a quarter of an hour.*

When the prayer was over and the transformation of her face had disappeared (as well as the ecstasy), Bernadette got up and wanted to leave the grotto. I stopped her for a moment and asked her to show me her left hand. I examined it with great care and found no trace of a burn. I then asked the person who had the candle to light it again, and I placed the flame of the candle several times under Bernadette's left hand, who quickly pushed it away, saying, "That burns me! I refer to this fact because I saw it, as did other people who placed the candle while I was near Bernadette.

The miracle of the candle seems to have occurred on an earlier occasion. According to J. B. Estrade, *my sister remembers that when Bernadette's fingers were on the flame of the candle, she could not stop screaming: "Take the candle away from the child! Can't you see it's burning? Your sister places this event on February 23rd.*

THE VISIONARIES

From April 7 to February of the following year, an unusual phenomenon occurred. Many visionaries claimed to have seen the Virgin. Some may have been moved by occult forces or by mental illness. The fact is that there were eccentrics, maniacs, hysterics and semi-crazy people who did strange and even grotesque things to attract attention. It seemed that the devil wanted to discredit the authentic apparitions, but these strange things soon disappeared and everything remained calm, since the grotto was a permanent place of pilgrimage. And the miracles that took place in the grotto confirmed the authenticity of the apparitions and made it more famous every day.

Bernadette, for her part, continued her normal life without trying to draw attention to herself. She went to school and prepared for her First Communion.... During recess she was still the cheeky and funny girl, laughing, singing and jumping with her classmates, although she was the most fervent during prayer time.

When she returned home, she often met pilgrims who wanted to talk to her and hear the story of the apparitions from her lips. On April 14, when people were talking about miraculous healings in the grotto, the imperial procurator,

Dutour, sent for Bernadette. She came with her mother. The procurator interrogated her for three hours. Bernadette herself told Sister Madeleine Bounaix: "We had been standing for three hours. I did not care about anything, but you can imagine the agony I felt for my poor mother. At the end of three hours, the Procurator's wife came and said to us: "Here is a chair, if you want to sit down. My mother said nothing, but I, who was in a bad mood, replied: "No, we would dirty it".

Another time, Bernadette will say that her mother finally sat down and she sat on the floor.

THE WATERS OF LOURDES

On May 4, the Prefect arrived in Lourdes, met with the Procurator, the Mayor and the Chief of Police, and ordered that all the devotional objects be removed from the grotto and deposited at the Mayor's office, where they would remain at the disposal of their owners.

It was decided that the water from the cave's spring should be analyzed to see if it had any curative properties and thus provide a rational explanation for the alleged miracles. The pharmacist Latour made the analyses and *discovered* that the water was very rich in chlorides, carbonates, silicates, iron oxides, soda sulfate, etc.. With this, the mayor thought of making a center of curative waters in order to have a good income. But first, in a meeting of the municipal council, it was decided to make a new analysis to confirm the results. This time it was done by Dr. Filhol, a professor at the Faculty of Science in Toulouse. The results were sent on August 8 and showed that Dr. Latour was a liar and had not done any analysis. He stated without any doubt that the water of the Massabielle cave was the same drinking water found in most of the springs in the area. Other pharmacists also carried out their tests, and all of them concluded that the water of the cave was natural, without any admixture of therapeutic substances.

For his part, on June 8, the mayor issued a municipal ordinance prohibiting entry to the grotto grounds; and a barrier was erected to prevent passage with a sign that read: *No entry to this property.*

FIRST COMMUNION

The First Communion in the hospice was set for June 3, the feast of Corpus Christi. The ceremony took place in the hospice chapel. Bernadette, like her companions, was dressed in white, with a veil on her head and a small hood over her shoulders. She made her First Communion with great fervor. Mr. Estrade's sister asked her:

- Tell me, which made you happier, receiving God or talking to the Blessed Virgin?

She replied: I don't know, both things go together and cannot be compared.
What I do know is that both times I was very happy.

Father Charles Laffitte says: *Bernadette had the grace of making her First Communion on June 3, 1858, the Thursday of Corpus Christi, with other young girls of her age. It is good to note that this blessed child, according to the testimony of the parish priest, who himself preached the preparation retreat, put all her care, modesty and respect into receiving it. From that moment on, there was another guarantee of Bernadette's sincerity. The edifying way in which she made her*

First Communion was a testimony.

After her First Communion, Fr. Pomian enrolled her in the Daughters of Mary group, which met in the hospice chapel.

SUMMARY OF APPEARANCES

To give a brief summary of the apparitions, let us look at what Bernadette wrote to Father Gondrand in 1861: *One day I went with two other girls to the banks of the Gave to collect firewood. Suddenly I heard what sounded like a noise. I looked at the meadow, but the trees did not move. Then I raised my head toward the grotto and saw a woman dressed in white, with a sky-blue belt and a yellow rose on each of her feet, the same color as the beads of her rosary.*

Thinking I was deluding myself, I rubbed my eyes. I reached into my pocket for my rosary. I wanted to make the sign of the cross, but I could not bring my hand to my forehead. When the Lady made the sign of the cross, I tried to make it too, and although my hand was shaking, I managed it. I began to pray the Rosary while the Lady was saying her beads, but without taking her lips off. When I finished the rosary, the vision disappeared.

I then asked the two girls if they had seen anything. They said they had not and asked me if I had seen anything. I told them that I had seen a woman dressed in white, but I didn't know who it was. I asked them not to tell anyone. They told me not to go back, and I refused. On Sunday I went back because I felt that I was being urged. ....

The lady spoke to me for the third time and asked me if I wanted to go for two weeks. I said yes, and she added that I should tell the priests to build a chapel there. Then she told me to drink from the well. When I saw no well, I went to the river Gave, but she pointed out that she was not talking about that river and pointed to the well. I approached it and found only a little water in the mud. I stuck my hand in and could hardly get anything out, so I began to dig, and finally I was able to get some water out; three times I threw it in, and the fourth time I was able to drink. Then the vision disappeared and I went away.

I went there again for fifteen days. The Lady appeared to me as usual, except for one Monday and one Friday. She always told me to warn the priests to build her a chapel, told me to wash in the fountain and pray for the conversion of sinners. I asked her several times who she was, and she replied with a faint smile. Finally, raising her arms and her eyes to heaven, she said to me: "I am the Immaculate Conception.

At that time He also revealed three secrets to me and absolutely forbade me to tell them to anyone, which I have faithfully obeyed to this day.

On the day of Corpus Christi, there were more than six thousand pilgrims in the grotto. And the healing of a child suffering from poliomyelitis took place. After placing him naked under the water jets of the fountain, he was dried and after a short time he began to walk without any effort. Dr. Dozous certified it as a miracle that happened before his eyes and before more than a hundred people who were direct witnesses.

LAST APPEARANCE (July 16)

On July 16, the feast of Our Lady of Mount Carmel, the 18th apparition took place. On that day, the stonemasons, gathered behind their banner, celebrated the feast of their patron saint.

In the afternoon, Bernadette, who had worn the scapular of Carmel since her First Communion, heard the Virgin's call again. She told her aunt Lucila and went to the grotto with a small group. They arrived at eight o'clock in the evening. They could not approach as before because of the barriers, but after praying a few Hail Marys, the Virgin Mary appeared. Bernadette said: *She greets us and smiles at us over the fences. Then she explained: She appeared to me in the usual place without saying anything to me. I had never seen her so beautiful.* So he said goodbye to her. It was her last appearance.

When her friends asked her, "How can you see it from the meadow if it is so far away? She replied: *I could not see the Gave or the tablets. It seemed to me that there was no more distance between me and her than at other times. I could only see her.*

News of the events at Lourdes had reached the Imperial Palace in Paris, for on July 28th the grotto was visited by, among others, Madame de l'Admiral Bruat, aide to the Imperial Prince, and Mr. Louis Veuillot, editor-in-chief of the important Catholic newspaper *Univers.* Both will publicize the events of Lourdes throughout France and obtain the removal of the barriers that have prevented access to the grotto. In the second week of September, Lourdes received an order from the Ministry of the Interior to remove the barriers and police surveillance.

A CONVERSION

Count Bruissard himself tells the story: "*I was in Cauterets when there was so much talk about the apparitions of Lourdes. I did not believe in the existence of God; I was an unbeliever and, worse, an atheist. I had read in a local newspaper that Bernadette had had an apparition on July 16 and that Our Lady had smiled on her. I decided to go to Lourdes as a curious person to see if I could catch the little girl in the act of lying.*

I went to the Soubirous house and found Bernadette at the door, busy darning some stockings. After a long interrogation about the apparitions, I asked her:

- *Let's see, how did this beautiful lady smile?*

The shepherdess looked at me strangely, and after a short silence, she told me

-   *Oh, Lord! You must be from heaven to smile like that.*

-   *Couldn't you do something like that for me? I am an unbeliever and I don't believe in your visions.*

The girl's face darkened.

-   *So, sir, you think I'm a liar?*

I felt disarmed. No, Bernadette was not a liar, and I was almost on the verge of falling to my knees to beg her forgiveness.

-   *Since you are a sinner, I will imitate Our Lady's smile.*

The girl rose very slowly, clasped her hands and smiled a heavenly smile such as I had never seen on mortal lips. Her face was filled with a disturbing reflection. She was still smiling, her eyes looking up to heaven. I remained motionless in front of her, convinced that I had seen the Virgin smiling through the face of the visionary.

Since then I have kept this divine memory in the intimacy of my soul. I have lost my wife and my two daughters, but it seems to me that I am not alone in the world. I live with the smile of the Virgin.

EPISCOPAL COMMISSION

On July 28, 1858, the Bishop of Tarbes, to whom the city of Lourdes belonged, formed a commission to investigate the events in the grotto. In addition to some clergymen, he invited some professors of medicine, physics, chemistry, geology, etc. ....

Canon Arnaud Fourcade, secretary of the investigatory commission, writes in his report *L'apparition a la Grotte de Lourdes* (Tarbes, Fouga, 1862): *She has been questioned by people from all walks of life, believers and non-believers, priests, prelates, military men, men of letters. She has been questioned by people from all walks of life, believers and unbelievers, priests, prelates, military men, men of letters. Sometimes she was asked difficult questions and puzzling objections, but she always amazed them with the speed and clarity of her explanations and answers.*

A learned man asked her how the apparition appeared, if it was surrounded by a halo. Not understanding the word "halo," she turned to a clergyman who was present to explain the meaning of the word. After explaining it to him, he answered without hesitation that the beautiful lady was surrounded by a soft light.

The interviewer asked her again if the halo appeared before or during the apparition. She replied that the light always preceded the apparition and that the halo followed the apparition after the light had disappeared.

Another person asked her in what language she was speaking to her. She replied that it was in patois (not French) *and when he remarked that this was not possible, that it was ridiculous, that the Queen of Heaven could not speak patois, Bernadette replied with a smile: "She cannot ignore any language. She spoke to me so that I could understand her, and I knew nothing but patois".*

A third person remarked to her that it was not worthy of the Blessed Virgin to have ordered her to wash her face with mud and eat grass. She replied that this was only a test of her obedience and that there is no one who has not eaten spiced herbs (salad).

She belongs to a poor family. Sometimes

rich people have offered her silver coins, gold coins, jewels and valuables, and she has refused them all. A pious lady, very rich, who knew her delicacy, put two gold coins in her pocket. How many people have offered to replace her poor clothes with more suitable ones, but she never wanted to exchange them!

Monsignor Garsignies, Bishop of Soissons, who was passing through Lourdes, wanted to see her and asked her to accept his silver-plated rosary. To encourage her to accept it, he told her that it had been blessed by the Holy Father. But, as if she had vowed not to accept anything, she stubbornly refused, respectfully thanking the prelate.

She has never been proud of the favor she has received. She speaks of it without the slightest affectation, without the slightest appearance of self-love.

When, in October 1859, Bernadette went to the waters of Cauterets on the orders of her doctors, Mr. Azun de Bernetas declared: "*She suffered with sorrow all the expressions of esteem that people showed her. Some asked her for something of hers, a medal or other object; but she replied: "I am not a merchant. She usually spent the day at her aunt's house without going out. Her recreation was to have fun with the two and three year olds at home. She only went out in the morning for Mass. She did not speak to anyone about the apparition unless asked.*

UNEXPLAINED HEALINGS

The same secretary of the investigative commission, Arnaud Fourcade, wrote in a minute some cases of humanly inexplicable healings. The first case is that of Louis Bouriette of Lourdes, cured in 1858.

Luis, 22 years old, and his brother José were working in the quarry, busy making a hole to put gunpowder to explode some rocks. The gunpowder exploded prematurely. Luis's face was burned and his right eye was severely injured by a piece of stone. This accident caused him great suffering and he had to stay in bed in a straitjacket for three months because he was delirious from the great suffering. His cerebral nervous system was in a constant state of irritation, he was attacked by madness for almost two years. He improved little by little, but when he wanted to start working, his right eye had very weak vision. The eye was almost lost. Hearing of the wonders of the water of Lourdes, he sent his daughter to the grotto to fetch water. As soon as she applied it to her eye, she saw a light, two hours later she could distinguish objects and he assured her that she would have been able to read with some difficulty. On the third day, after washing himself with the water of the cave, he saw as perfectly as if he had never had the slightest accident. And with this healed eye he saw better than with the other, which was not injured. He was convinced that the Blessed Virgin Mary, Mother of God, had given the water of the grotto the power to heal.

Two years after his recovery, Luis was summoned by the Commission of Inquiry to certify his recovery.

Another case. Croixine Duconte, 38 years old, a neighbor of Lourdes, testified under oath before the Commission on November 17, 1858, that her two-year-old son had been habitually ill since shortly after his birth; and she was already thinking of finding means to bury him, as he was cadaverous in color and hardly breathing.

Croixine spoke to her husband about taking her son to the cave to immerse him in the water. The husband hesitated, believing that the child would not be able to bear the fatigue of the journey, but he agreed because his son seemed incurable. They arrived at the cave, where there were many people. The mother immediately immersed the child in the pool of water, to the astonishment of the people for such an act of cruelty in the middle of winter. After praying, she returned to the village. When she got home, she put the baby in the cradle and the baby slept peacefully until the next morning without any breastfeeding or other nourishment. In the morning, the baby woke up and asked to be breastfed and asked to get up as if he wanted to walk, which he had never done before. She kept him in the cradle, but the next day, after he had slept peacefully, when she got him up, the child walked for the first time in his life with the greatest ease, to the amazement of his father, mother, relatives, and neighbors. Since that day, the child has not had the slightest complaint. Dr. Vergez, who examined him on June 27, 1860, recognized the supernatural nature of this sudden healing under the conditions described.

Father Peyramale, the parish priest of Lourdes, wrote a letter to Secretary Fourcade of the Investigation Commission on May 17, 1860, in which he informed him of about a dozen healings that medical science could not explain.

In another letter dated November 2, 1860, he wrote: *Last Wednesday, October 31, a lady from Garlin came to thank Our Lady of the Grotto for the cure of her husband. Her husband was in despair, vomiting blood and having unbearable pains in his intestines and head. Seeing that all the remedies he had taken were ineffective, she put a cloth soaked in the water of Lourdes on him. At the second compress, the illness disappeared as if by magic, the patient fell asleep and woke up completely cured.*

CONFIRMATION

On February 5, 1860, the Bishop of Tarbes, Bishop Laurence, arrived in Lourdes. Bernadette and many of her companions were confirmed. Master Jean Barbet recounted a funny scene. Sister Marie Géraud, who was preparing her for confirmation, heard whispering and laughter in a corner of the room. Bernadette stood up and said that she was the guilty one; because the doctor had forced her to take tobacco for her asthma, she had offered it to her neighbors. They pretended to take it and started sneezing, so they burst out laughing.

His brother Jean-Marie explained in the

ordinary trial of Nevers: *I often brought him tobacco to the Lourdes hospice, and I also sent it to Nevers, because the tobacco of Lourdes is finer than that of Nevers.* Also in his hospice cupboard he had some white wine on medical advice.

After confirmation, he was allowed to receive communion every eight days, which was very unusual in those days.

HOSPICE RESIDENT

Since so many pilgrims came to Lourdes, they did not leave Bernadette alone, as many wanted to see her and talk to her. So the parish priest talked to the director of the hospice, Ursula Fardes, so that she could be admitted as a guest and continue her studies. In this way she would receive free food and lodging and be somewhat safe from unwelcome people who wanted to see her. In mid-July 1860, she was accepted as a boarder. She was placed in a separate room, cheerful and healthy, and was given a special place at the boarders' table. The costs were covered by the municipality, so the mayor also gave the go-ahead.

In the hospice there was a free school for

the poor on the first floor, and on the second floor there were two classes, one for pensioners who paid five francs a month and the other for those who paid two francs a month. Bernadette was assigned to the two-franc class, even though she paid nothing. At the beginning of the school year, the retired students were excited to learn that the visionary was going to separate the classes of the poor from their own. Bernadette was saddened by this demotion. For her, her place was among the poor and she expressed her desire to continue with them.

Catherine Fourcade explained: *When they wanted to put her in the pensioner class, she refused, saying that she did not want to leave the free class, that she wanted to be better off in the second class; and she was placed in that class as she had requested.*

Her rapid progress was soon seen, for on May 28, 1861, she wrote an account of the apparitions to Father Gondrand in French and with good penmanship, although with some spelling mistakes. As for her behavior, the nuns agree that she was *very obedient, a good companion, very edifying, with a very cheerful and sometimes mischievous character.*

Her sister Antoinette (Toñita) says in her testimony at the trial: *Bernadette always had a good hand with sewing and embroidery; she knitted, crocheted and mended.*

Let's look at some anecdotes: One school day in strawberry weather, says her friend Julia Garros: *It was hot and the windows were open. We looked at the strawberries under the window with a certain greediness. Bernadette said, "I'm going to throw my shoe in the garden. You go get it and bring us strawberries." And Juliet replied, "Said and done.*

Another day she showed her stubbornness, but her classmates did not notice. One Sunday she was ordered to change her dress and refused to obey because she wanted to visit her parents, as she had been promised since the day she entered the convent. On another occasion, Sister Victorina surprised her by lengthening her skirts to give them the appearance of a peekaboo. On another occasion, at the suggestion of a companion, she inserted a piece of wood into her corset. Perhaps she got carried away with a bit of female vanity, but it soon passed without a trace. It was a kind of childish prank to imitate her friends.

In the chapel, she was admired by all for

her fervor in praying the Hail Mary's and especially for making the sign of the cross as the Virgin Mary had taught her. Her confessor allowed her to receive Communion frequently, and even when she was sick, she refused to drink water so as not to break her fast, which at that time began at midnight of the previous day, in order to receive Communion. She loved to receive Communion in a special way and prepared herself well to receive it. Even in the most painful moments of the asthma crisis, after sleepless nights, she would get up to go to Communion. At night she was given some pills to calm her cough. But she would tell me, "No, I would fall asleep with the pill in my mouth and I would not be able to go to Communion.

She usually went to the cave twice a week, accompanied by a nun, to visit her family. In the cave, she drank water from the well and kissed the ground. Then she prayed devoutly and inconspicuously. Those were her happiest days. At the hospice, the nuns sometimes allowed some people to talk to her. She would go to these visits against her will. *We would say to her: "Why are you leaving? And she would answer: "Because they send me.*

People who visited her would ask her for a

souvenir, even if it was just a hair, but she would totally refuse. If they gave her stamps to sign, she would accept them and write p.p. Bernadette, which meant *Priez pour Bernadette* (Pray for Bernadette). Because of this, her classmates teased her by calling her *pepé Bernadette.* By this time, she could speak French and answered all questions in French.

Sister Victorine Poux says that a Carmelite priest from Bagnères went into the kitchen to see Bernadette and knelt before her. Bernadette was washing her hands. When the priest knelt down and said to her, "Bernadette, bless me," she replied, "I cannot bless. Then say, "Holy Virgin, you who have appeared, bless the Father." And Bernadette repeated it.

Sister Victorina adds: *I have seen her cry when there were 20, 30 or 40 people in the hall waiting for her. Big tears would roll down her cheeks. I would say to her: "Have courage. She wiped her eyes before entering and greeted them graciously and answered their questions.*

The visits made her tired and she sometimes complained. The nuns insisted that the apparitions were not for her pleasure, but for the good of the whole world.

Occasionally she was asked to touch her rosaries. She would do this by taking them in one hand and touching them with the other, without giving it any importance, in order to get rid of people. But Father Pomian forbade her and she never did it again. When they were presented to her to touch, she would reply: "I have been forbidden to do so"[89].

Bernadette prayed the rosary several times a day and recited it before going to sleep. <She did not try to attract attention. She made the sign of the cross like everyone else, but if she thought she was not being seen, she would do it slowly, with dignity.... She was very devoted to praying the Rosary and was seen praying it many times a day. She would pray it before going to bed. And she would say: "I pray the rosary every day for those who entrust themselves to my prayers. She was simple and cheerful with her companions and participated in their games. She loved to take care of the sick in the hospice (where there was a hospital). According to Sister Victorina: "She had no money and was averse to it. To those who wanted to give her something, she would say: "Here is a piggy bank for you"; or she would take my hand and give it to me.

STATEMENT BY THE BISHOP OF TARBES

The Commission of Inquiry into the events of Lourdes was still in progress. Before making the conclusions official, Bishop Laurence wanted to hear Bernadette's testimony in person. All the members of the commission were present in the sacristy of the church of Lourdes. She appeared in her usual simplicity, wearing clogs and her cap. According to witnesses, she spoke with impressive assurance and authority. As she repeated Mary's words: *I am the Immaculate Conception, she lowered her hands, raised her eyes, and seemed to be enveloped in a supernatural clarity. The elderly bishop was moved and said after the meeting, "Have you seen this child?"*

The Bishop of Tarbes, in his public declaration of the authenticity of the apparitions, on January 18, 1862, stated: *Many were cured by the waters of the grotto, many of diseases that had resisted all medical treatment. These extraordinary healings had tremendous resonance. The echo spread far and wide. How many sick people were healed and how many families were comforted. If we wanted to give their testimony, countless voices would rise to proclaim the sovereign efficacy of the water of the grotto. It is not possible to list all the benefits obtained, but it is certain that the waters of Massabielle have cured patients declared incurable. These cures were obtained by using water that, according to chemical tests carried out after rigorous analysis, had been deprived of any natural curative properties. Some cures were obtained immediately, others after using the water two or three times, either as a drink or as a lotion. Furthermore, these healings are permanent. These healings are God's work. The apparitions were the starting point. There is a close relationship between the healings and the apparition.*

The apparition is divine because the healings have the divine seal. Therefore we say: "The finger of God is here".

The seven healings approved as miracles by Monsignor Laurence on January 18, 1862, were the following

1. Catherine Latapie de Loubajac, cured on March 1, 1858, of cubital paralysis due to traumatic elongation of the right brachial plexus.
2. Louis Bouriette of Lourdes, cured in March 1858 of trauma to the right eye.

3. Blasina Cazèna of Lourdes, cured in March 1858 of chemosis or chronic ophthalmia.
4. Henry Bousquet of Nay, cured April 29, 1858 of fistulized adenitis.
5. Justin Bouhort of Lourdes, cured on July 6, 1858 of chronic post-infectious hypotrepsia with motor retardation.
6. Magdalena Rizan de Nay, cured of left hemiplegia, October 17, 1858.
7. Maria Moreau de Tartas, cured on November 9, 1858, of a very marked loss of sight with inflammatory lesions in the right eye.

On that occasion, Monsignor Laurence also declared the apparitions authentic, saying

We judge that the Immaculate Mary, Mother of God, truly appeared to Bernadette Soubirous on February 11, 1858, and 18 times in the following days, in the grotto of Massabielle, near Lourdes. This apparition has all the characteristics of truth and the faithful are authorized to believe it to be true. We humbly submit our judgment to the Sovereign Pontiff, who is responsible for the government of the universal Church.

Article 2.- We authorize the veneration of

Our Lady of the Grotto of Lourdes in our diocese, but we forbid the publication of any special formula of prayer or hymn or devotional book relating to the apparitions without our written consent.

Article 3.- In order to carry out the will of the Blessed Virgin, manifested several times during the apparitions, we propose to build a sanctuary on the grounds of the grotto, which will be the property of the Bishops of Tarbes.

Many people went on pilgrimage to Lourdes in search of healing. Those who could not travel were desperate for water from the grotto. The parish priest of Lourdes, Peyramale, wrote to Bishop Laurence on August 21, 1862: *We are asked for water* (from Lourdes) *from everywhere, not by the bottle, but by the ton. A director of the Major Seminary of the Ardennes wrote to me yesterday that he had used up many cases of water that I had sent him. He asked me to send him a barrel to satisfy all the requests.*

DEATHLY ILL

After the apparitions, Bernadette wanted to become a religious, but she did not see this possibility very closely, since she was often sick with asthma and vomited blood because of the tuberculosis that had manifested itself. Sometimes her asthma attacks were so severe that she would say: *Open my chest!* [95]. *On the other hand, she* did not know which congregation to choose and did not have the necessary dowry to enter.

On April 20, 1862, after visiting the grotto, he became seriously ill and was in danger of dying. The last rites were administered to him. Father Pomian gave her a small piece of the host for communion, and at that moment she felt better and asked for water from the grotto. She drank a few drops and exclaimed: *I am cured.* The next morning the doctor returned, thinking she was dead, and found her perfectly well. He thought it was because of the medicine he had recommended, but was told she had not taken it.

About this event, the parish priest, Father Peyramale, wrote a letter to Canon Fourcade on April 30, 1862. In it he wrote: *Bernadette had been suffering from a very serious case of pneumonia for several days. Last Sunday, April 27, she was very ill, causing the sisters great concern. They blamed themselves for letting her go to the grotto, where they thought she had contracted the disease. On Monday she got worse. She was coughing a lot and breathing with great difficulty. Immediately after receiving Communion, Bernadette felt healed. She experienced a relief as if a mountain had been removed from her chest. Her alarming symptoms disappeared, and yesterday morning she saw the family doctor, Dr. Balencie. The doctor was amazed. He attributed the cure to the effectiveness of the remedies he had prescribed. Unfortunately, Bernadette did not take them and did not recover. ....*

I forgot to tell you that in order to make it easier for Bernadette to receive Communion, I gave her some drops of water from the grotto. Since I had been told that the doctor had taken the pneumonia for a nervous condition, a rather serious mistake, Bernadette said: "If I am sick again, I would ask the doctor to be more careful not to mistake one illness for another, because I could be dead because of the illness I had.

IMAGE IN THE GROTTO

On September 17, 1863, Joseph Fabisch, professor of sculpture at the Lyon School of Fine

Arts, arrived in Lourdes. He had been asked to make a statue of the Virgin as Bernadette had seen her. That same day, the sculptor wrote to his wife: *"We went to see the young girl, who answered all the questions I asked her to clarify how to do the work. I have never seen anything more beautiful than when I asked her who the Virgin was and she said: "I am the Immaculate Conception. She stood up with great simplicity, folded her hands and raised her eyes to heaven. Neither Fiésole, nor Perugino, nor Raphael created anything so gentle and at the same time so profound as this young girl's simple look.... I shall never forget this charming expression as long as I live. In Italy and elsewhere I have seen the works of great masters who have managed to reproduce the impulses of divine love and ecstasy, but in none of them have I found such softness and charm.... And every time I have asked him for this expression, he has done it in the same way.*

The sculptor's daughter Antonia, then a child, explained in the trial: *I remember that my father's stay in Lourdes, the first time, was a ray of sunshine in his existence. He came completely enlightened. He recounted with faith and enthusiasm all that he had seen and heard. His devotion to the Blessed Mother was renewed. Every night my father would take a rosary and pray the whole thing, which I believe he does to this day.*

The picture was finished in Lourdes on March 30, 1864. It was made of pure Carrara marble. The inauguration and blessing of the image was scheduled for April 4, the feast of the Annunciation, since March 25 was Good Friday. In the afternoon, in the presence of the Bishop of Tarbes, there was a solemn procession with 20,000 people and 200 priests.

According to the vicar general of the diocese, Monsignor Fourcade: *"The image is admirable. It reproduces with scrupulous fidelity the moment when the Virgin raises her hands to the height of her breasts and her eyes to heaven and says: "I am the Immaculate Conception.*

But when Bernadette was asked what she thought of the image, she replied: *"It is very beautiful, but it is not Her. And when asked if it is possible to imagine the beauty of the Lady by looking at this sculpture, she said, "Oh, no. The difference is as from earth to heaven. The difference is as from earth to heaven.*

PREPARING THE ENTRY

On September 25, 1863, the bishop of Nevers visited her. At that time she was in the kitchen washing vegetables. The bishop spoke to her and she answered him in correct French. The bishop asked her:

- *What are you going to do with your future?*
- *"Well, nothing."*
- *What do you mean, nothing? Something must be done in this world.*
- *"I am here with the sisters."*
- *But she is here on a temporary basis.*
- *"I wouldn't mind staying forever."*
- *But you are not a sister, which is a prerequisite for a permanent stay. Shall I find you an easy and comfortable job in the world?*
- *"Ah, not that."*
- *Why not become a sister?*
- *"You know that I am poor and will never have the necessary dowry. Besides, I am good for nothing.*
- *Recently, in the kitchen, I realized that I am good for something. Think about it and tell Mother Superior to tell Mother General or me, and I will take care of the rest.*

The bishop spoke personally to Mother General,

who objected: "*Monsignor, Bernadette is not in good health. She will always be a pillar of the infirmary.* (Here Mother General was wrong, for she could embroider very well and also had the charisma to care for the sick with love).

- *She will always be able to peel carrots, as I saw her doing in the kitchen.*
- *If you ask us, we will give it to you.*

Bernadette herself, on August 15, the Feast of the Assumption, went to Mother Alexandrina and told her: "Dear Mother, I am determined to become a religious and if the Reverend Mother General will accept me, I will be very happy to enter this congregation.

From that day on, Bernadette was welcomed into the community events and embroidered a very beautiful album that was admired by all. Seeing that she had a special gift for caring for the sick, she accompanied Mother Alexandrine on her visits to the sick in the hospice hospital. She confided in Jeanne Vedère: *I love the poor very much, I like to take care of the sick; I am going to stay with the Sisters of Nevers. They have given me a sick person to take care of; when I am well, no one will take care of him but me. I will stay with them.*

But she was not yet officially admitted. Mother General replied to the Bishop of Nevers that she would be received when she was in good health, since she had been in very poor health since the winter of 1864. She spent almost a year in this condition and was admitted as a postulant at the end of 1865, along with another young woman, Leontine Mouret.

In 1866, shortly after Easter, she went directly to the novice mistress, Mother Therese Vauzou, who was then replacing Mother General, to ask her to accept her as a religious in the Congregation.

On May 19, 1866, Monsignor Laurence, Bishop of Tarbes, consecrated five altars in the crypt, the foundation of the future chapel of the Sanctuary of Lourdes. The next day, a large crowd of thousands of faithful flocked to the grotto. There was a solemn procession led by the bishop. Bernadette was there and the people waved to her. *She was happy as an angel and dressed in her dress as a daughter of Mary. Some servants surrounded her.*

The nuns had to separate her because they wanted to cut off her dress as a relic. Faced with this, she only said: "What fools!

After returning from the grotto, many people went to the hospice to see it. They had to close the gates, and some still climbed the walls. The soldiers had to help keep order. Mother Ursula Court had Bernadette come and go along the gallery so they could see her from a distance. She was upset and said to the superior, "You are showing me off to everyone as if I were a freak.

ENTRY INTO RELIGIOUS LIFE

Her departure from Lourdes was scheduled for July 4, 1866. On July 3, accompanied by some nuns, she entered the grotto for the last time in her life. There she sighed and exclaimed: "*My mother, my mother, how can I leave you?* She rose to place her lips on the rock and then on the rosebush. Then the superior said to her: *We must go.* Bernadette replied, "*Just for a moment. This is the last time.* And she quickly wiped her eyes and walked back to town.

Mother Alexandrina said to her: "*Why are you so sad? The Blessed Virgin is everywhere, and everywhere she will always be your mother.*

- *Oh yes, but the cave was my heaven.*

She spent the night with her family. The next day, her mother, on her father's arm, Toñita, twenty years old, Juan María, fifteen, Bernardo Pedro, seven, and some aunts accompanied her to the hospice, where they all said goodbye, crying, except for her. She told them: <You are very good, but I cannot stay here forever.

He was 22 years and three months old. He entered the Congregation of Charity and Christian Instruction in Nevers. At the time of his entry, the Congregation was in full bloom. The community in Nevers, both in the novitiate and in the house, had 132 novices and 30 postulants, in addition to a large number of professed sisters. *When Bernadette arrived, according to Sister Lucia Cloris, she did not differ in any way from the other postulants, except perhaps because she was too shy.*

The day after her arrival, all the postulants, novices and professed gathered to hear the story of the apparitions for the first and last time. At times, Bernadette did not know what to say. The story was shorter than ever before. *Only through questions, which she answered briefly, were we able to hear a brief summary of the truth we already knew.*

NOVICIADO

On July 29, 1866, along with 44 other postulants, she received the veil and habit of a novice. On that day, the novice mistress, Mother Thérèse Vauzou, did not give her a new name, as was customary, but her baptismal name: Sister Marie Bernarda (Marie Bernarde). When she prayed the Rosary, she was transformed. Her companion, Anastasia Carrière, noted: *One could say that she saw the Blessed Virgin as in Lourdes.*

In her studies she was behind in mathematics and spelling, but gradually she improved. As a novice, she was an assistant in the sacristy and infirmary. As assistant to the head nurse, she devoted herself with great care to the care of the sick, but soon her health began to fail and at the beginning of September she was confined to her bed. From her bed, she participated in the activities of the community, especially during Mass and the community prayer. She used to say many ejaculatory prayers throughout the day as an easy and simple way to pray continuously. In mid-October she was very ill, and the novices took turns praying for her health. *For many days a large number of candles burned without ceasing for her.*

She received extreme unction in view of her very serious condition and expressed her desire to make her religious profession *in articulo mortis.* Mother General consulted her councilors and they agreed to receive her. One day the doctor assured her that she would not live through the night. The bishop was urgently informed and came to hear her profession in person on October 25, 1866.

Bernadette, with a little whisper in her voice, said that she could not pronounce the formula of her vows. The bishop did so on her behalf: *I, Sister Mary Bernadette, desiring to consecrate myself to the service of God and to the works of charity in the Congregation of the Sisters of Charity and Christian Instruction, established in the Diocese of Nevers, take the vows of poverty, chastity and obedience in the manner explained in the Rule of the Congregation itself, approved by the Sovereign Pontiff. I pray to our Lord Jesus Christ through the intercession of the Blessed Virgin, my Mother, to grant me the grace to faithfully fulfill these vows. And she answered with all her heart: Amen.*

Immediately, the superior general placed the black veil on her forehead and placed the crucifix of profession in her hands, leaving the rosary and the book of the Rule on her bed. As the Bishop and the Vicar General withdrew, Bernadette regained her voice, and as everyone waited for her last breath, she came to life; and turning to Mother Teresa, the novice mistress, she said *I will not die tonight.*

After sleeping for a few hours, she awoke at four in the morning and told her nurse: "*Sister Emilia, I feel better. God did not love me. I got to the door and she told me: "Turn around, it's too soon.*

From that October day, she began to improve. The doctor forbade her to return to normal life until the intense winter cold had passed, but she could attend chapel, visit the Blessed Sacrament, and walk a little in the cloister. However, she was to be confined to the infirmary. She remained there from August 14, 1866 to February 1867. Since she was an enemy of idleness, when she was not in prayer, she did some simple work or read a book. Her favorite readings were on the Eucharist and the Passion of the Lord. And especially the New Testament and the Imitation of Christ. Sister Marcelina explained: *I loved to see her pray because she prayed like an angel. When she received Communion, I discovered the love she had for Our Lord. Her eyes remained lowered, her face paled and was transformed: she looked heavenly. It was the same when she was asked to pray the rosary in the novitiate or to console those who were sad.*

She resumed her normal novitiate life with her white veil because she had to repeat her profession with her companions. The novice mistress, Mother Teresa, looked for all her faults and often humiliated her on purpose. As Superior General, she said to Mother Bordenave, her secretary: "*I do not understand why the Blessed Virgin appeared to Bernadette. There are others who are so nice, so well educated.*

Sometimes he treated them coldly, thinking that was the best way to keep them humble, but he made them suffer. A companion said: *I remember very well that the novice teacher was very strict with her. She reprimanded her with harsh and short words. You could see her turn pale, but she never made a move or uttered a word of discontent. One day, to one of her companions who complained that she was being treated so harshly by the mistress of the novices, she said: "Well, I owe her deep gratitude for the good she has done to my soul.*

RELIGIOUS PROFESSION

Bernadette prepared to make profession with all her companions, since she had made her profession *in articulo mortis* and it was felt that it should be renewed. Of the sixty novices, only forty-four were accepted for profession. The ceremony took place on October 30, following a seven-day retreat. All were professed for one year. In the afternoon, according to custom, all the professed received their Letters of Obedience, that is, the assignments for the works and places to which they were destined, and, kneeling, they also received the crucifix, the rosary, and the book of the Rule.

When it was Bernadette's turn, the superior general said to the presiding bishop, "This daughter is good for nothing. The bishop said: "I give her the task of praying". In fact, she was given the job of assistant to the director of the infirmary, Sister Marta Forès. It was a great satisfaction for the patients of the hospice to be cared for by her.

FRANCO-PRUSSIAN WAR

On July 15, 1870, during the First Vatican Council, the Franco-Prussian War broke out. An outpatient clinic with 20 beds was set up in the hospice. Bernadette was very attentive to the wounded. The bishop asked her for special prayers to protect the city. When she heard that the Prussians were approaching Nevers, she said: "I am not afraid of them. God is everywhere, even among the Prussians. I am only afraid of the bad Catholics.

On December 9, the whole city of Nevers was alarmed. She writes:
Our officers were wounded and, fearing that they would be taken prisoner, they fled. They placed cannons on the terrace of the convent and the sisters had to agree to keep eight horses in the stables. The social situation was very tense, but she was calm. She wrote to her sister Antoinette: "My health is quite good. There is only one thing we have to do: pray a lot to the Blessed Virgin so

that she will intercede with her Son and obtain her forgiveness and mercy for us. I am confident that God's justice, which is now punishing us, will be softened by the intercession of our tender Mother". On January 28, 1871, the armistice was signed and the war ended.

DEATH OF THEIR PARENTS

On December 10, 1867, while the first procession in honor of Mary Immaculate was making its way to the crypt under the grotto, she was informed that her mother had died on the eighth at the age of 41. Bernadette exclaimed: *I rejoice, for she is in heaven.*

On March 4, 1871, her father died at the age of 64. Sister Madeleine Bounaix said of this event *At about half past seven, I went to the infirmary of St. Catherine and found our dear Sister Marie Bernarda leaning against the fireplace and crying. I knelt down beside her and asked her: "What is it, dear sister, did I upset you unintentionally? She replied, "Oh, no, about two weeks ago you had a bereavement - one of my brothers had died - and I consoled you; today it is my turn, I have just heard of my father's death.*

He died on Saturday at nine o'clock. Sister," she added, "always be very devoted to the Sacred Heart of Jesus, because it is a great consolation when you lose one of us and you are absent, to think that you have prayed for him. That is what I did on Saturday night: I prayed for those who were dying, I prayed for my Father who was entering eternity.

According to Father Sempé: *He was a simple and upright man, a good man and full of faith. When he was dying, he joyfully showed the scapular he was wearing. For many hours and until his last breath, he did not stop praying.*

The apparitions of Lourdes and having a saintly daughter had made him, like his wife, a good Christian, leaving behind the vices of his past life.

NURSE AND SACRISTAN

In 1871, the head nurse became seriously ill and Bernadette took charge of the infirmary. First on loose sheets of paper, then in a prescription book, she wrote a memorandum to remember, without fear of being mistaken, the obsolete measures used in medicine, such as grains, scruples and ounces. For example: 1 grain was equal to 5 centigrams, 3 scruples were equal to 1 gros or 4 grams, 1 ounce was equal to 32 grams. He made a list of the pharmacy's inventory and, in the opinion of all, carried it out with seriousness and responsibility.

She treated the sick with affection, but did not compromise the established norms. One day, Sister Julienne Capmartin, a novice in 1872, was in the infirmary with a bad cold. He gave her hot tea, covered her well, drew the curtains and advised her to stay quietly under the blankets to sweat. But Sister Julienne stretched out one arm and then the other, took the book of the Office of the Virgin and began to pray. When Bernadette saw her like this, she said to her in a stern tone: *Here is a devotion sewn with disobedience.* He took the book from her and wrapped it up again.

Sister Anne-Marie Lescure was blind and had breast cancer. The disease was so disgusting that Sister Vicenta Garros said she, who was Bernadette's assistant, could not even look at it. It was a large, deep wound full of maggots that would fall and Bernadette would pick them up in a bowl. She would heal it with great delicacy. And she would say to Vicenta: *What kind of Sister of Charity are you going to be?* She also said to her one day when she had doubts about dressing a dead woman: *You coward, you will never be a good Sister of Charity. A Sister who cannot touch the dead, what good can she be?*

On November 5, 1872, the matron died after a long illness, and Bernadette officially took over. But by January 17, 1873, she was already ill with asthma abscesses and had to stay in the infirmary as a sick person. In April she recovered somewhat, but in May she relapsed again. On June 3 she received the last rites for the third time in her life. When she recovered, she was removed from her position as Sister and given the job of Assistant Sacristan. She liked this job, too, *so that she could decorate the altar of the Virgin and be close to Our Lord.*

On Christmas Eve, *after finishing the crib, she took the baby Jesus to put him in his place. She was heard to say: "How cold you must have been in the manger of Bethlehem, my little Jesus. Those people had no heart when they refused you hospitality; but I am glad that I prepared this manger for you!*

PERSECUTIONS AGAINST CATHOLICS

Devotion to Our Lady of Lourdes and pilgrimages increased. In 1872, Father Sempé, the parish priest of Lourdes, wrote *24 processions arrived at the grotto with incomparable joy and edification. But hell was on the move. The press multiplies its blasphemies, in the streets the Marsellaise is sung. In Fleurance* (Gers) *the banners were burned. In Cette, the brave pilgrims of Nîmes are persecuted with ignoble insults. In Perpignan, it was forbidden to go to the station in procession, but the persecutions and obstacles increased the fervor of the pilgrims a hundredfold. Roussillon sent three pilgrimages and prepared others. Gers is multiplying its own. Cette organized a second one, composed of men only. Niort, following the example of Poitiers, set in motion the entire Potou region, the Vendée and the neighboring regions. They came in haste, fearing that tomorrow's storm would cut short their pious journey. In the grotto they prayed, sang and shouted with enthusiasm: Long live the Immaculate Conception and long live Pius IX!*

But the revolutionary anti-Catholics were not satisfied. Unable to stop the flow of pilgrims to the grotto, they tried to slander Bernadette. A professor at the Salpêtrière University propounded the theory that it was all a hallucination, and the newspapers repeated his ideas, saying that Bernadette was mad in the convent of the Ursulines of Nevers.

The courageous bishop of Nevers had to respond and say publicly:

1. *Sister Maria Bernarda has never set foot in the convent of the Ursulines of Nevers.*
2. *She lives in Nevers at the Motherhouse of the Sisters of Charity and Christian Instruction, where she entered and where she remains free.*
3. *Far from being mad, she is a person of extraordinary intelligence.*

I would like to invite the illustrious professor, whose name I do not remember, to come and personally verify the accuracy of my statements. I will put him in touch with Sister Maria Bernarda. And so that you have no doubt as to her identity, I will ask the Procurator of the Republic to present her to you in person. And he will be free to question and contradict you as long as he wishes.

Another pretended deception against the Catholic religion was the sale, with all possible publicity, of a liqueur with the title: "Immortal

Divine Liqueur of Lourdes, composed by Father Félisse". The leaflet bore the picture of the apparition with these words: "To Our Lady of Lourdes. Miracle of February 11, 1858. A magnificent bottle sealed with a miraculous medallion commemorating the miracle of Lourdes and illustrated with a drawing of the apparition of the Blessed Virgin to Bernadette Soubirous. This delicious liqueur is made with water from the "miraculous spring of Lourdes".

The bishop informed the manufacturer that the title of the liqueur, the brochure, the medal... were an insult to religion and a deception of the public. And that the Bishop of Tarbes, owner of the source of the grotto, formally forbade the drawing of water to make any liqueur and that he would rigorously prosecute any violation of this prohibition.

CONTINUE THEIR ILLS

By October 1875 he was in very poor health and unable to work. She had to remain in the infirmary and spent her time reading and praying. Some postulants and novices visited her from time to time. One day, two postulants who had come from Lourdes showed her a photo of the grotto. She simply said: "*Oh, how much the poplars have grown! <Another day, Sister Philippine Molinéry showed him another picture of the grotto to see how he would react. Suddenly she said to him*

- *Do you know what the broom is for?*
- *To sweep.*
- *And then what do you do with it?*
- *He puts it behind the door.*

Well, this is my case. The Blessed Virgin used me and then put me in my place. I'm happy and I'm staying there.

One day, *the newly arrived Miss Dahlia said to Mother Bernadette Berganot: "I've been here for three days and I still haven't found Bernadette." "Look at her," she said. I was so disturbed," said Bernarda Dalias, "that I could not keep an inappropriate word from my lips, and I exclaimed: 'This?*

Bernadette, who heard him, took his hand with a beautiful smile and answered in a jovial tone: "Yes, Mademoiselle, I am nothing more than that". With these words he conquered the postulant's heart, and she summed up what she thought of herself.

133

From time to time, during his solitary time in the infirmary, he went to the grotto in his mind. *One day Sister Aurelia Gouteyron asked him: "Wouldn't you like to see the street again? And he replied, "I would like to be a little bird so that I could see without being seen. Every day I go with the thought of making a little pilgrimage.*

Sometimes, *when he was very thirsty because of fever, he would say: "It will be a small mortification that I will offer for the souls in purgatory. She never asked for a sedative.* Sister Marcellina Lannesssans said: "*I liked to see her pray. She prayed like an angel.*

On some occasions she would *say the prayers aloud, repeating, "My Jesus, have mercy. My God, I am all yours. I love You. Convert sinners.* Sister Bernarda Dalias affirms: *The Holy Eucharist was the breath of her soul.*

Her gaze on the host was *very impressive*. Sometimes, to give her Communion, it was necessary to *wait a little while for her asthma to pass.* Sister Vicenta Garros said to him: *"How can you spend so much time giving thanks? And she replied: "I believe that the Blessed Virgin is giving me the Child Jesus. I receive him, I talk to him, and he talks to me".*

Sister Victoria Cassou explained that *one Christmas night he was at her side and was able to observe her. After Communion, she went into such deep recollection that when we all left, she did not notice. I stayed by her side because I did not want to celebrate Christmas Eve with my companions. I looked at her for a long time. Her face seemed radiant and heavenly, as in her Massabielle ecstasies. When the sister in charge of locking the doors went to fulfill her mission, she made a great noise with the keys. Then Bernadette came out of that ecstatic state. She left the chapel and I followed her. She came up to me and asked me politely, "Have you had anything to drink?" I replied, "No, and neither have you." And she withdrew quietly, and we parted.*

On the other hand, it was his custom every morning to commend to the Christ of Sorrows the souls of those who would die that day.

The Rosary was her favorite devotion. She loved the pictures of the Blessed Virgin through which she manifested her love for her. One day, Bernadette was alone in the infirmary, dusting the fireplace. Sister Clara Bordes watched her through the crack in the door. *Bernadette picked up a statue of Mary, kissed its feet and returned it to its place. Then she stood motionless before it, her hands resting on the edge of the fireplace, her gaze fixed on the image. She remained in this posture for five minutes.*

By June 1876, Bernadette had lost the use of her legs and was brought to Mass in a wheelchair. She had a severe cancerous abscess in one knee. Despite the pain she was in and the sacrifice she made for sinners, she said: *I am happier in my bed with my crucifix than a queen on her throne.*

The Bishop of Nevers was about to make an *ad limina* visit to Pope Pius IX in Rome, and thinking that the Pope would ask him about Lourdes and Bernadette, he asked her to write a letter to the Pope. She wrote it on her bed. Sister Gabrielle de Vigouroux testified that she held the folder for him while he wrote. In that letter she told the Pope: *My weapons are prayer and sacrifice, which I will keep until my last breath. Then the weapon of sacrifice will fall, but the weapon of prayer will accompany me to heaven, where it will be more effective than in this exile. I ask the Sacred Heart of Jesus and the Immaculate Heart of Mary to keep you among us for a long time, because you make them known and loved by us. It seems to me that every time I pray for your intentions, the Blessed Virgin looks down from heaven on you, Most Holy Father, since you proclaimed her Immaculate Conception; and four years later, this exalted Mother came to earth to say: "I am the Immaculate Conception". I did not know what she meant. I had never heard those words before.*

Then, thinking about it, I said to myself: "How good the Blessed Virgin is! It can be said that she came to confirm the word of our Holy Father".

However, when the draft of the letter written by Bernadette was presented to the General Council, it seemed to them that the style was not up to standard and they decided to have her rewrite it in a more solemn, elevated and distinguished tone. The Pope gave Sr. Maria Bernarda (Bernadette) *a silver crucifix, which he made me kiss respectfully,"* said Sr. She was *confused to see that the Holy Father was so attentive to her.*

On June 8, 1877, the feast of the Sacred Heart of Jesus, a procession was held through the convent courtyards. Bernadette slowly followed the procession on crutches. At about six o'clock in the evening, a terrible storm broke out and lightning struck very close to Bernadette's bed, setting fire to some of the ornaments kept in the sacristy. *Frightened, Sister Casimira Callery approached Bernadette and said to her: "Don't worry, it is the devil who is upsetting our beautiful feast".*

When Sister Casimira Callery said goodbye to her on October 27, 1877, she told her that it was more like a farewell. She said to him: *"Seraphim, when you hear of my death, pray for me, for it will be said: This "saintoune" (holy woman) does not need you, and I will be left to drink in purgatory.*

PERPETUAL PROFESSION

After eleven years of first annual vows, Bernadette was to make her perpetual vows. The ceremony was held on September 22, 1878. She made her perpetual vows with 61 other companions and confided to Sister Marta du Rais: *"I imagined that I was already in heaven. If I had died then, my salvation was assured, because the vows became a second baptism.*

How much he loved priests! On October 4, 1878, a 17-year-old boy, Jean-Marie Febvre, who was about to enter the seminary, visited his cousin, the chaplain of the convent. The superior and the chaplain arranged for him to meet Bernadette. *The Superior said to Bernadette, who was walking slowly: "Sister, go to the back wall of the garden and get a bunch of grapes for this young man who has just arrived from a long journey.*

He points: *When he offered me the grapes he had picked for me, he asked me:*

139

- *Do you want to be a priest?*
- *Yes, Sister, if God calls me.*
- *You will be a priest. How beautiful it is to see a priest before the altar!*

The priest before the altar is Jesus Christ himself on the cross. You will have to work and suffer. Have courage!

DEATH

Since 1867 or 1868 he had been suffering from a white tumor on his right knee. During the winter of 1877 the condition worsened. By now the tumor had reached enormous proportions, causing him constant pain. At the same time, his weakened bones were suffering from tooth decay.

Mother Teresa Bordenave explained: *Her sufferings were so intense that the nuns wasted their charitable efforts trying to calm her down with so many tortures. The sick woman's face became sallow and she seemed to be dead. She spent the nights without sleep, and when she was able to sleep for a few moments from exhaustion, the sharp pains woke her up immediately to martyr her without rest.*

Her right leg had to be constantly propped up on a chair in front of the bed. Sometimes she would let out a moan that she tried to stifle, but without screaming. And she would say: *"In my sleepless hours I am happy to be united with Our Lord. A picture of a monstrance was placed on the curtains of her bed. And he said: "A glance at this prayer card gives me the desire and the strength to sacrifice myself when I am beset by loneliness and suffering.*

On March 18, 1879, her sister Antoinette and her husband Joseph Sabathé visited her. She was so ill that she could only speak to them with signs and her eyes. The next day, the feast of St. Joseph was celebrated with great solemnity in the convent. She told Father Febvre that she had asked him for the grace of a good death. He received the last rites for the fourth time in his life. After receiving communion, Bernadette asked all the sisters for forgiveness for the bad example she had given. She added: "Especially for my pride.

On April 14, she was tempted by Satan. She said, "Go away, Satan. Go away, Satan. The next day she told the chaplain that the devil had tried to attack her, but she invoked the name of Jesus and regained her confidence.

On Tuesday, April 15, she had the strength to receive Communion. Father Febvre granted her a plenary indulgence *in articulo mortis* (at the moment of death). In the evening, Mother Adelaide Dons, then Superior General, was praying in the chapel, kneeling before the altar of Our Lady and praising Bernadette. Suddenly she seemed to hear an inner voice urging her to go upstairs to the infirmary. From the threshold she heard an anguished cry: *"Sister, sister. I am afraid. I have received so many graces. I appreciated them so little. The mother said to her: "All the merits of the Sacred Heart belong to us. Offer them to God in payment of your debts and in thanksgiving for all His benefits. "Oh, thank you," she replied, and she was relieved.*

On Wednesday, April 16, she continued to suffer. At one point he stretched out his arms and looked at the crucifix: "Oh, my Jesus, how I love you. Then, looking at the picture of Our Lady, he exclaimed: "I saw her, I saw her. How beautiful she was. How I long to see her again.

In her last moments, Bernadette asked for the letter containing the special blessing of Pope

Pius IX for the hour of her death. She was told that in order to receive it, it was enough to have the intention and to pronounce the name of Jesus. This she did immediately.

At about a quarter past three o'clock, she took the crucifix in her hands and slowly kissed the five wounds. A few moments earlier she had said: "My God, I love you with all my heart, with all my soul, and with all my strength. Three sisters at her side kept repeating: "Jesus, Mary and Joseph, have mercy on her and protect her.

Near the end of his agony, he cried out: "*My God, my God.... I am thirsty*. One of the sisters offered her water and moistened her lips. And in a last effort, she made a majestic sign of the cross. Her last words were: *Holy Mary, Mother of God, pray for me, poor sinner...poor sinner.*

Sister Gabrielle de Vigouroux said: "*I arrived in time to receive her last sigh, which she gave very sweetly, leaning on my arm. She had the crucifix in her hand, pressed to her heart. I think it was even tied. She was lying on her right side. I remember having trouble closing her right eye, which kept opening.* When she died, she was 35 years, three months and nine days old.

As soon as she died, *Bernadette's face was pale and calm with an expression of purity and beatitude.* The sisters dressed her in her religious habit. Sister Gabriela Bigouroux explained: "*It was not difficult for us because her body was supple, even though she had been dead for two hours. Her body was taken to the chapel and laid out, surrounded by white hangings and lilies, with a crown of white flowers on her black veil, her rosary in her hands, her crucifix and the formula of her perpetual vows between her fingers. Bernadette seemed to be asleep.*

When they heard the news, they all exclaimed with one voice: *She was a saint. She had ascended to heaven to return to the Blessed Virgin.* For two days her body was exposed to the people. Four sisters took turns touching her body with objects of piety given to them for this purpose, such as medals and small crosses. .... Her funeral took place on Saturday, April 19. None of her relatives were able to attend. In a unique exception, Bernadette was not buried in the city cemetery, but in the garden chapel dedicated to St. Joseph.

SAINT JOSEPH AND HIS ANGEL

Bernadette had a devotion to many saints, but especially to St. Joseph. *During the bad days of the dark night of the soul, when she was afraid of death, she prayed to St. Joseph, who is the patron saint of a good death.*

She piously celebrated the month dedicated to St. Joseph (March). *We had placed a picture of the saint at her bedside, which she decorated with flowers and before which two candles burned. We recited the litanies and all the prayers to St. Joseph that she knew. Sometimes I would say to her: "Here we are.*
Don't you know any other prayers? And he would answer me: "No, we have already said them all. He assured me that he had received many graces through St. Joseph.

One day he was in the infirmary and promised a sick woman that he would pray for her. He said to her, "Are you suffering? Wait a little while, I am going to visit my father." "Your father?" "Yes. Don't you know that my father is now St. Joseph?

He made many novenas. Once I noticed that while he was making a novena to the Blessed

Mother, he was kneeling before an image of St. Joseph. I told him, "You are wrong. You pray to the Blessed Virgin and you kneel before St. Joseph." He said to me: "The Blessed Virgin and St. Joseph are in perfect harmony, and in heaven there is no envy".

In the records of the beatification process, one of the nuns explains that she often repeated the invocation: *St. Joseph, give me the grace to love Jesus and Mary as they wish to be loved. St. Joseph, pray for me and teach me to pray.*

Among the saints, after St. Joseph, she had a special devotion to St. Bernard, the second patron of baptism (Maria Bernarda). Also to St. Francis of Assisi. Since the constitutions of the convent forbade her to belong to the Third Order of St. Francis, she had the cord of her order imposed on her. She received it in the infirmary on December 8, 1878, from the Capuchin missionary Manuel Touzelier.

She was also very fond of her guardian angel. *One day she suggested to Sr. Vicenta Garros: "When you pass in front of the chapel, if you don't have time to stop, ask your guardian angel to take your errands to Our Lord who is in the tabernacle. He will have time to take them to*

*Him and then He will come back to you". So far I
have followed this custom.*

*Sometimes I would say to him: My angel, I
ask you to go where my Jesus rests. Tell this kind
prisoner of love to come to my heart and make it
his dwelling place.*

SUPERNATURAL GIFTS

Among other gifts, she had the gift of
prophecy. *In May 1870, Sister Angela Lompech
received a letter from home informing her that
her mother was at death's door because of her
ninth childbirth. She began to cry. Bernadette
found her crying and asked her why. She replied,
"I just heard that my mother is very sick. Maybe
she is already dead." Bernadette looked at her
with a smile and said, "No, don't cry. The Blessed
Virgin will heal your mother." "I was comforted
and I stopped crying. Soon after that, another
letter arrived saying that the sick woman was out
of danger. I later learned that the improvement
had begun at the same time Bernadette had told
me: "Do not cry. My mother lived another thirty-
seven years.*

Anne Durand, a postulant from Nevers,

had to go to the infirmary to have her eyes treated. Bernadette was also there and greeted her warmly. Anne confided in her her grief at being told that she would have to return home. *But Bernadette assured her that she would be a sister of the same congregation. She told her: "The Blessed Virgin will heal you". In fact, she became a nun under the name of Marcelline Durand and became the superior of the hospital in Tulle.*

One day in May 1872, a 25-year-old woman in high society dress appeared in the parlor. She had run away from home because she wanted to become a nun and her parents would not give her permission. She was accompanied by a maid who also asked for permission to enter.

The superior general was puzzled because her father had done everything possible to take her away, either by degree or by force. <Faced with this desperate situation for the postulant, Bernadette said to her: "God wants you here and you will not move in spite of all the opposition". In fact, the father's anger gave way and he accepted his daughter's vocation. This young lady became Mother Martha de Rais, Superior of the House of Providence in Montmartre and member of the Legion of Honor, as she testified in her

cause for canonization.

She also had the gift of healing the sick. Mother Maria Teresa Bordenave assures us that *during her lifetime it was common knowledge in the community that she achieved several healings through her prayers. In June 1862, when she was 18 years old, a gentleman and a lady arrived from Cauterets with a sick girl. They asked the prioress of the hospice to allow Bernadette to touch their daughter, believing that she would be cured. The prioress called Bernadette and asked her to fix the little girl's pillow. She did so, and the next day the girl was much better and was able to go to the cave on her own.* This first event was included in the beatification process, according to Mother Teresa Bordenave's testimony.

Sister Vicenta Garros, for her part, testified: *A strange woman brought to Lourdes a son of hers, about a year old. The poor child's face and head were full of evil. On the fourth day of a novena to Our Lady of Lourdes, the woman presented herself with the child in the hospice. The child was crying. She entrusted him to Bernadette, who took him around the convent and returned to give the completely healed child to his mother. All traces of evil had disappeared.*

Another day, a lady with a sick child had the idea of giving Bernadette a crocheted, tangled and unfinished crib blanket to unravel. The concierge, Sister Victoria Cassou, gave it to Bernadette to mend and it was Bernadette who did the finishing work. She brought it back and the good lady put it on the child and he was cured.

On another occasion, says Sister Clara Bordes, *a lady brought a child who could not walk to be touched by Bernadette. Mother General, Josephine Imbert, asked Bernadette to take care of him while she spoke with his mother. She did so. She took the child in her arms and then, because he was very heavy, she put him on the ground. The child was healed and ran happily to his mother.*

LOURDES AND BELGIUM

Among the Catholic nations, Belgium has been the one that has been most distinguished for its devotion to the Virgin of Lourdes from the beginning. On June 29, a grotto similar to that of Lourdes was inaugurated on the outskirts of Ghent. It is the Grotto of Oostaker, where many miracles have begun since 1873. Among the many miracles that took place in this artificial grotto of Oostaker in Belgium, is that of Peter van Rudder. On February 16, 1867, he broke his leg in a fall from a tree. The stumps were separated by a hole of about three centimeters. His suffering lasted eight years because he did not want to have his leg amputated, as the doctors told him.

On April 7, 1875, he went to the Oostsker Grotto with his wife. When he arrived in front of the image, he felt a kind of convulsion running through his body, dropped his crutches and knelt before the image, something he had not been able to do for eight years. According to a later medical report, the gangrenous wounds had healed and the tibia and fibula, which had been separated by three centimeters, had rejoined. Welding of the bones was complete and the legs were the same length again. During the 23 years that he lived in good health, the doctors unanimously confirmed that the fact was inexplicable to science. This case was recognized as a miracle by the ecclesiastical authority after the medical verdict of inexplicable to science. It is the 24th miracle recognized in Lourdes.

A GREAT MIRACLE

We refer to the spectacular miracle that occurred before the eyes of Dr. Alexis Carrel (1873-1944). It happened in July 1903. Dr. Carrel, a disbeliever, replaced one of his companions to go as a doctor on a pilgrimage of 300 sick people to the sanctuary of Lourdes.

He did not believe in God or in miracles. He was a scientist who believed only in reason, but he was a sincere man, and at the end of the journey he must have realized that God and the supernatural existed. He tells us about his spiritual adventure in his book *Journey to Lourdes*, where he writes his impressions under the name of Dr. Lerrac (the reverse of Carrel).

It reads: *The train stopped before entering the station at Lourdes. The windows were filled with pale, ecstatic, joyful heads, in a salute to the chosen land where evil would disappear.... From these desires, these fears and this love, a great longing for hope was born.*

When the sick arrived at the hospital, Lerrac approached the bed of a young woman suffering from tuberculous peritonitis..... Marie Ferrand (her real name was Marie Bailly) had ribs marked on her skin and a swollen abdomen. The swelling was almost uniform, but a little more voluminous on the left side. The abdomen seemed to be distended by hard matter, and in the center there was a more depressed area filled with fluid. It was the classic form of tuberculous peritonitis. .... The father and mother of this young woman died of consumption; she has been vomiting blood since the age of fifteen; and at the age of eighteen she contracted tuberculous pleurisy and had two and a half liters of fluid removed from her left side, then she had pulmonary cavities, and finally she has been suffering from this tuberculous peritonitis for eight months. He is in the last stage of cachexia. The heart beats without order or concert. She will die soon, she may live a few days, but she is doomed.

Maria Ferrand, after some ablutions with the miraculous water of the Virgin, because her condition was extremely serious and they did not dare to put her in the pool, they took her to the image of the Virgin in the grotto.

Lerrac's eyes fell on Maria Ferrand and it seemed to him that something had changed in her appearance, that her complexion was less pale.... Lerrac approached the young woman, counted her pulse and respiration, and remarked:

"Breathing is slower. Obviously, a rapid improvement in the general condition was before his eyes. Something was about to happen and he refused to get carried away. He concentrated his gaze on Maria Ferrand without looking at anyone else. The face of the young woman, her eyes bright and ecstatic, fixed on the grotto, was still changing. There had been an important improvement. Suddenly, Lerrac felt pale when he saw how, in the place corresponding to the waist of the sick woman, the cover was gradually dropping to the level of the belly....

The clock in the basilica had just struck three o'clock in the afternoon. A few minutes later, the tumefaction of the belly seemed to have completely disappeared.... Lerrac did not speak or think. This unexpected event contradicted all his ideas and predictions, and he seemed to be dreaming. A cup of milk was given to the young woman and she drank it in its entirety. After a few moments, she raised her head, looked around, stirred a little, and lay back on her side without the slightest sign of pain. It was about four o'clock.

The impossible, the unexpected, the miraculous had just happened! This tormented girl, who had been on the verge of death, was almost cured.

It could not be nervous peritonitis, Lerrac thought. The symptoms were too pronounced and too clear.... Around half past seven he returned to the hospital, burning with curiosity and fear.... He was speechless with amazement. The transformation was amazing. The young woman, wearing a white shirt, sat up in bed. Her eyes shone in her face, still gray and haggard, but mobile and alive, with a rosy color in her cheeks. The corners of her lips, when at rest, still bore a painful line, the mark of so many years of suffering, but from her whole person emanated an indefinable serenity that radiated around her, illuminating the sad room with joy.

- Doctor, I am completely cured," she told Lerrac, "although I feel weak.... The cure was complete. That dying woman, with a cyanotic face, a distended belly and an agitated heart, had in a few hours become an almost normal young woman, only emaciated and weak. ....
It is the miracle, the great miracle, that makes the crowds vibrate, that attracts them madly to Lourdes!
What a happy coincidence to see how, among so many sick people, the one I knew best and had watched for so long was healed!

INCORRUPT BODY

One of the things that strikes visitors to Bernadette's tomb in Nevers is the miraculous preservation of her incorruptible body, displayed for all to see in a glass urn.

The first exhumation to examine her body took place on September 22, 1909, after thirty years of burial. She was found to be beautiful and without any signs of decomposition. The flesh, parched and intact, retained its whiteness. The head was covered with a headdress and a veil; the hands were crossed on the chest, holding the crucifix (rusty) and the rosary, which were completely moldy. The eyes were closed, a little

156

sunken in their orbits, and the lips were half open, as if in a smile.

The second exhumation took place on April 3, 1919, and the third on April 25, 1925. Dr. Comte stated: *The body is intact.... There is no sign of the usual and normal cadaveric decomposition after a long stay in an open grave in the ground.* On this occasion the face was blackened. For this reason, his face and hands were covered with a film of wax to enhance his features with natural colors.

One of the miracles approved for his beatification was the cure of Henry Boisselet, who had been suffering from tubercular peritonitis since November 1913 and was cured on December 8 of that year. The other was that of Sister Maria Melania Meyer. In 1910, at the age of 30, she vomited a lot of blood and was diagnosed with an ulcer. Unable to eat, she was so malnourished that her early death was feared. She was taken to Bernadette's tomb in St. Joseph's Chapel and was completely cured.

She was beatified by Pope Pius XI on June 14, 1925 and canonized by the same Pope on December 8, 1933. Her feast day is April 16, the day of her death.

LOURDES TODAY

Lourdes is currently one of the most important Marian sanctuaries in the world and where most miracles take place. Every year about six million pilgrims visit it. *One of the characteristics of Lourdes is that there is an international commission of doctors who examine the cases of possible miraculous healings. So far they have considered 67 cases as inexplicable to science, which the Church has officially declared as miracles. There are also 7,000 files of extraordinary healings that are to be studied. Of course, every year there are thousands of extraordinary cases; but for any cure to be considered inexplicable to science, it must have many demanding requirements. That is why only 50 new cases that meet the conditions are studied each year.*

If a person believes he has been

miraculously healed, his file must be examined by the permanent doctors of Lourdes. He is then invited to appear before the Commission the following year and in subsequent years. If the various examinations are favorable, the case is referred to the International Medical Committee, created in 1947 and composed of 30 specialists, surgeons, professors or attachés from different countries, who meet once a year. Like a court of appeal, the International Medical Committee upholds or rejects the position taken by the medical office of first instance. Decisions must be made by a large majority. If it is considered medically inexplicable, the case is referred to the Bishop of the place where the cured person resides, who must establish a diocesan commission composed of priests, canonists, and theologians. And it is up to the bishop to definitively declare whether or not the cure is to be considered miraculous.

The last miraculous healing in Lourdes, the 67th, was that of Anna Santaniello, an Italian woman who had suffered from a heart defect since childhood that doctors had declared incurable. At the age of 40, she was unable to walk or speak clearly and had cyanosis in her face and lower limbs. She lived to be over 90 years old in perfect health. This miracle was officially recognized on November 11, 2005, after a commission of doctors from Lourdes declared her healing inexplicable to science.

Lourdes is the town of miracles. It is the city of God, where the presence of God and spiritual values are strongly felt. It is the city of Mary, because Mary appears as the Queen of the place, who leads everyone to unite with God in the Eucharist. For this reason, many prefer to call it the city of the Eucharist, because Jesus is especially present during the Mass for the sick and when the sick are blessed with the Blessed Sacrament.

On summer evenings it is very beautiful to see thousands and thousands of people of every race, language and nation singing together the Hail Mary and praying the Rosary during the torchlight procession, each one with his candle in his hand. It is a glorious moment in which, on the night of Lourdes, it seems that the stars of heaven come down to earth to pay homage to Jesus and Mary, as on that Christmas night. And God responds by performing spectacular miracles and, above all, by giving peace to all the pilgrims.

We can say that Lourdes is a beacon of faith in this unbelieving world. It is a city of prayer and peace. And after Rome, the Catholic city par excellence, along with Fatima and Guadalupe in Mexico, it is one of the most important shrines in the world.

Personally, I have been to the Shrine of Our Lady of Lourdes only once in my life, and I can testify that the finger of God is there. There is a religious atmosphere that touches the soul. I was filled with strong emotions, especially at night during the torchlight procession, praying the rosary and singing in different languages. In the morning, it was very moving to see the large crowds of people who came to invoke Mary to ask God for her intercession. There were many sick people in wheelchairs, accompanied by the *volunteer nurses*. Many certainly hoped to be healed, but all without exception went away comforted in their faith and with great spiritual strength to carry on with their cross on their shoulders and to accept their vocation to pray for the conversion of sinners.

Pope John Paul II called on the Church to celebrate the World Day of the Sick every year on February 11.

FINAL MESSAGE

St. Bernadette was Mary's messenger to give the world a message of light in the darkness, to give faith to those who no longer believed in the supernatural. The main message that God wanted to give to the world through Mary and with the help of Bernadette was to pray for sinners. To make us think that this life is fleeting and that we should think of the eternity that awaits us. That life passes quickly and there is a whole eternity, happy or unhappy. And that is why we should give more importance to the things of God than to the things of this world, to spiritual things than to material things.

The Virgin Mary clearly told Bernadette that she would not be happy in this world, but in the next. Therefore, we too must live in the perspective of eternity. Concerned at the same time for the salvation of others. Not to think only of feasts, pleasures and amusements. God allowed sufferings and illnesses in the life of St. Bernadette so that she would have much to offer for sinners, for poor sinners who are the poorest of the poor because they do not have God and the peace of God in their hearts.

In conclusion, let us take note of Mary's message: live for eternity and offer our good works, sufferings and illnesses for the salvation of those who live in sin and are in danger of eternal damnation. Let us take life seriously and live for eternity.

May God bless you through Mary.

SPECIAL THANKS

Thank you so much for purchasing our book! We hope you and your loved ones are enjoying it. If you have a moment, we would greatly appreciate it if you could leave a review on Amazon. Your feedback helps us improve and helps other customers make informed decisions.

Here's how you can leave a review:

- Log in to Your Amazon Account: Use the same account you used to purchase the book.
- Go to Your Orders: Hover over the "Accounts & Lists" tab at the top right of the page and click on "Your Orders" from the dropdown menu.
- Find Your Purchase: Scroll through your orders to find the book you purchased.
- Leave a Review: Click on the "Write a product review" button next to the book title.
- Rate and Review: Choose a star rating and write your review. Please share what you enjoyed about the book and how it met your expectations.

Your honest review is invaluable to us and helps our book reach more readers who will benefit from it.

Thank you again for your support!

Sor Anna Garavitt

BIBLIOGRAPHY

Azun de Bernétas, *La grotte des Pyrénées*, Larrieu, Tarbes, 1961.

Bordenave Maria Teresa, *La confidente de l'Immaculée, Bernadette Soubirous*, 1912.

Carrol Alexis, *A Journey to Lourdes*, Ed. Iberia, Barcelona, 1988. Courtois Gaston, *Lourdes*, Ed. Fleurus, 1958.

Cros Léonard, *Histoire de Notre-Dame de Lourdes*, 3 volumes, Ed. Beauchesne, Paris, 1926 and 1957.

Cros Léonard, *Notre Dame de Lourdes. Recits et mystères*, Ed. Privat, Toulouse, 1901.

Dozous Pierre-Romaine, *La grotte de Lourdes, sa fontaine, ses guérisons*, Paris, 1874.

Estrade J.B., *Les apparitions de Lourdes, Souvenirs intimes d'un témoin*, Tarbes, 1909.

Fourcade Arnaud, *L'apparition à la grotte de Lourdes en 1858*, Fouga, Tarbes, 1862.

Guynot, *Sainte Bernadette. Souvenirs inédits*, 1936.

Lasserre Henri, *Bernadette, Soeur Marie Bernard*, Palmé, Paris, 1879. Lasserre Henri, *Notre Dame de Lourdes*, Palmé, Paris, 1869.

Laurentin René, *Lourdes. Documents authentiques*, 7 volumes, Lethielleux, Paris, 1957-1966.

Laurentin René, *Le sens de Lourdes*, Lethielleux, Paris,

1955.

Laurentin René, *Lourdes. Histoire authentique des apparitions*, 6 volumes, Lethielleux, Paris, 1961-1962.

Positio super virtutibus, Private Edition of the Sacred Congregation of Rites, Rome, 1922.

Apostolic process of Nevers. Archives du couvent de Saint-Gildard. Apostolic process of Tarbes. Archives du couvent de Saint-Gildard. Ordinary process of Nevers. Archives du couvent de Saint-Gildard.

Procès ordinaire de Tarbes. Archives du couvent de Saint-Gildard. Ravier, *Écrits de sainte Bernadette*, Lethielleux, Paris, 1961.

Schwob René, *Capitale de la Prière, Lourdes*, Descleé de Brouwer, 1934.

Sempé and Duboé. *Notre-Dame de Lourdes par ses premiers chapelains*, pp.

Sempe et Duboé, Letouzey, Paris, 1931.

Soubirous Bernadette, *Diario di una passione*, Ed. Interlinea, Novara, 1996. Trochu Francis, *Bernadeta Soubirous*, Ed. Herder, Barcelona, 1958.

Trochu Francis, *Sainte Bernadette, la voyante de Lourdes*, Vitte, Lyon, 1954.

Made in the USA
Columbia, SC
22 November 2024

47363058R00100